MR. MARCH

Calendar Boys Series

NICOLE S. GOODIN

Mr. March
Published by Nicole S. Goodin
ISBN: 978-0-9951168-5-6
Copyright 2019 by Nicole S. Goodin
All rights reserved. ©
First published March 2019

Cover design by Nicole Goodin
Images purchased from Deposit Photos
Editing by Spell Bound

This book is a work of fiction. All names, characters, places and incidents either are products of the author's imagination or are used fictitiously. Any resemblance to events, places, or persons, living or dead, is purely coincidental.
The author acknowledges all song titles, song lyrics, film titles, film characters, trademarked statuses and brands mentioned in this book are the property of, and belong to, their respective owners.
Nicole S. Goodin is in no way affiliated with any of the brands, songs, musicians or artists mentioned in this book.

For all the babes born in March

CHAPTER ONE

Luke

I glance over at Mia as they begin to lower Troy into the cold, hard earth.

I've never seen a woman as broken as the one I see now, and I've seen a lot – more than any man should ever have to.

She's clutching her newborn son like a lifeline as she says her final goodbyes to her husband – the love of her life.

This grief – it's the price you pay for love.

Sobs wrack her small body to the point where I'm worried she'll drop Joe, the tiny baby my best mate will never, ever get the chance to meet.

He was *so* excited to be a father. He loved Mia like nothing I've ever seen before and he loved the baby growing inside of her just as much.

The two of them were one of those couples that you can't help but watch – you could literally see the love in their eyes when they looked at one another.

I've known the both of them since high school; they were childhood sweethearts who shared a love you would probably never find twice. Hell, I haven't managed to find anything like it even once.

That's what scares me the most I think... that Mia will never find that again and that Joe will never have the father he deserves.

I hate to think they'll be alone forever.

I catch Mia's eye and I watch her bottom lip tremble as everything she's ever known is ripped away from her.

She's looking right at me, but it seems like she's looking *through* me more than anything.

I know she doesn't blame me, but I couldn't fault her if she did. I couldn't save her husband when they brought him in to me, and I should have been able to. I wish more than anything I could have.

I'd have given anything for it to have been me that was struck with that stray bullet instead of him. I have nothing and no one who would mourn me as deeply as Mia is mourning Troy. He had the whole world waiting for him back home.

He had *everything* he ever wanted, and he was only a few days from getting it all.

He was getting out. We both were. Him to be a father, and me to pursue a different career path... a different life.

We both wanted a life *outside* of the Army.

We were *so* close.

He should have been there with Mia when she gave birth. Instead his body was in a box being flown home from the other side of the world.

I don't know how Mia will survive her life without him. He's all she's known for such a long time.

I know she's accustomed to being without him for long periods of time while we were deployed, but this is different. This time he's not coming back.

Up until he took his last breath, his only concern was for that of his family – his wife... his baby.

I made a promise to a man I respect far more than I respect myself, that I'd take care of her, *and* their son, for as long as they needed me too. No matter how long that might be for.

I might not have been able to save his life, but I *can* keep my word. I can dedicate my own life to them.

I can do that for him.

I never, ever break a promise and I'm not about to start now.

I crouch down next to the deep, dark hole, long after everyone else has gone and whisper into the darkness.

"I'll take care of them, Troy, I promise you."

CHAPTER TWO

Luke
Two years later

I sit down on the bottom step and wipe the sweat from my brow.

I swear this is the hottest day we've had all year and I'm spending it pushing around a lawn mower.

"Here."

I startle; I hadn't even heard her come up behind me.

Mia holds out a glass of her homemade lemonade for me to take.

I reach for it gratefully and chug it back in one go.

She sits down next to me, her tanned leg brushing against mine as she does.

She's got on the shortest pair of shorts you've ever seen and a tiny little singlet top.

I know she hates wearing such a small amount of clothing, but this heat is what it is. Even Mia can't cover herself up in these temperatures.

She smiles at me and holds up the jug to see if I want a refill.

I nod eagerly. Mia's lemonade is my favourite.

"You know, you don't have to keep mowing our lawn. I can get a guy in or do it myself…"

I down half the glass this time and chuckle as I wipe my mouth.

That lawnmower would easily weigh more than she does, so I'd be surprised if she could push it around out here for an hour. And as far as 'getting a guy in' goes, *I'm* the guy people get to mow their lawns.

This conversation is nothing new, we have this same discussion at least every two weeks – we have a lot of other discussions too. Whether it be about me fixing things for her, putting out her rubbish bin, mowing her lawn or cleaning out her guttering, she always feels needlessly guilty.

"You know I don't mind, Mia." I bump my knee against hers and she smiles sheepishly.

"Would you at least let me pay you?" she replies hopefully.

I roll my eyes. Same conversation, different day.

I swig back the rest of my drink and get to my feet. "What did I tell you yesterday?"

"That you'll never take my money," she grumbles.

I wouldn't take a cent from her. She's doing okay financially, but it's just her now. Troy isn't here to make ends meet for them anymore.

"Where's Joe?" I ask as I use the bottom of my shirt to wipe my face.

"I just put him down for a nap."

She smiles so sweetly at the mention of her son, and I thank the powers that be, yet again, for giving him to her. If it weren't for Joe, I don't know how Mia would have gotten through the past two years.

Truthfully, I'm not sure I would have managed without him either.

"Tell him I'll catch him later then, alright?" I call as I turn away and push the mower in front of me.

"You're still coming for dinner, right?" she asks.

I come for dinner every Tuesday and Friday, she knows this, yet every single week she checks.

I've not missed a dinner since she first invited me – I probably never will. As long as she wants me around, I'll be there.

"It's Tuesday, Mia." I chuckle. "I'll be here."

She doesn't answer, and I don't turn, but I can picture the blush staining her cheeks as though I was looking right at her.

I lift the mower onto the back of my truck and wave out to her before climbing in.

"Thank you, Luke," she calls to me. She's still standing up on the steps, the sun glistening on her golden hair like some kind of angel.

"Anytime, Mia."

I swallow the lump in my throat as I drive away down the street.

It's not easy seeing your best friend die before your eyes.

It might be even harder realising that you've got feelings for his wife.

***

I finish up my list of jobs for the day with plenty of time to spare. I never thought I'd wind up being a handy man around my neighbourhood, but here I am. In fact, I never thought I'd wind up living in suburbia, surrounded by house after house that looks just like mine, but sometimes plans change.

I thought I'd be travelling the world and when I finally did come home to settle down, it would be with a woman by my side, and as a medic, not a hammer hand, but after Troy, I just *can't*.

I can barely look at a stethoscope without breaking out in a cold sweat.

I can't listen to a ticking clock without being taken back to the moment when I frantically tried to hear his heart beating. I can't even visit a GP's office without giving myself a pep talk in the car before I head in.

And as for having a woman in my life, I guess I do – but not at all in the way I'd imagined.

Mia isn't the only one who broke inside the day he died – I came out more than a little worse for wear too.

I pull into my driveway and kill the engine on my truck.

I've got an hour to get cleaned up and get back to Mia's.

I need to make my usual stop on the way, and then I get to enjoy one of the best nights of my entire week with my two favourite people.

I'd never put much thought into having children of my own, but after hanging out with Joe these past couple of years, I can't imagine not having them one day.

He makes *everything* better.

He's a distraction, entertainer and love giver all wrapped up in one cute little package.

He's a really great kid. Mia is doing an incredible job of raising him.

I know Troy would be so proud of her. I hope he'd be proud of me too.

I've kept my word. I look after Mia and Joe in every way I possibly can. I'm there for Mia in any way she'll allow me to be.

I trudge up the stairs, stripping off my dirty, sweaty clothes as I go.

I turn the shower on, scalding hot – just the way I like it, and step under the steady stream.

The shower is the one place I let myself give in and think about Mia in the way I would if she were just some woman I'd met and not the widow of my closest friend.

If Troy really is up there somewhere, looking down on us, I'm pretty sure he'd step out and give me some privacy while I took a shower, so I figure I'm safe to fantasise in here.

I can't recall *when* it happened, but it's almost as though one morning I woke up and she wasn't *just* Mia, my friend anymore.

I don't only love her as a best friend. I'm *in* love with her too.

She's Mia, the *beautiful*, sexy woman with a laugh that makes me smile and a voice that I feel down to my bones.

She's funny, sweet, smart and broken.

And I love *everything* about her.

I don't know if it's the broken in me that loves the broken in her, but I do know I never, ever looked at her in this way when Troy was alive.

She's been Troy's since school, but he's not here now and I don't know what I'm supposed to do about that.

I don't *want* to be in love with her, and I've spent the better part of the last six months trying to convince myself that it's just a phase, or a crush that I'll move on from, but each time I see her, it only cements the fact that these feelings aren't going anywhere at all.

And every single day, I feel a little more guilty than I did the last.

CHAPTER THREE

Mia

There's a knock at the door at 6.00pm on the dot.

I don't know how many times I've told him that he doesn't need to knock anymore, but he never listens.

In fact, he never does anything I tell him.

He never stops doing things for me and Joe. He never stops spoiling my son with toys or day trips. He doesn't stop doing my yard work or fixing my car.

He never moves on from us and focuses on his own life.

He listens to all the important things I say, though. He hears me when I'm upset, or when I'm lying about being okay. He listens when I talk about Joe or my dreams of the future.

He knows me so well now. He's my best friend.

He might even know me better than I know myself these days. It's been a long two years, and if I'm honest I don't really know who I am anymore.

To most people, I'm a widow.

To Joe, I'm Mumma.

But to me... I just don't know.

Everything I had planned for my life has changed. It all changed the minute his light went out and faded into darkness.

The only thing I'm certain of is that the man waiting on the porch will be there to support me through it all. All I have to do is ask.

I open the door and sure enough, Luke is standing there waiting, a bunch of flowers in his hand.

"For you," he says as he holds them out to me with a smile.

I still don't know why he does this, but it's a tradition spanning nearly two years at this point, so I don't bother acting surprised the way I used to.

Luke has been here for me, *whenever* I've needed him. Nothing is ever too big of an ask or an inconvenience.

He was here with me, changing nappies and heating bottles when Joe was only tiny and I was sleep deprived and struggling to manage on my own.

He was the only one I trusted to hold my baby without supervision for a long time.

He was here through storms, power outages and broken windows.

He's *always* been here.

I know he thinks it's Joe who has gotten me through, and while I don't know what I'd do without my son, it's *him* that held my head above water and made sure I didn't drown.

I owe a lot to the man in front of me.

I hold my hand out for the flowers and bring them to my nose to breathe in the sweet, floral scent.

"They're beautiful, Luke, you didn't have to."

"I wanted to," he replies – like he always does, with a shy smile.

"Thank you."

"Wuke!" the little voice behind me shouts.

Luke's eyes light up at the sound of my son's voice.

I've never seen a man so smitten with a child before. They share a bond that goes well beyond friends. It cuts me deep that the closest male role model Joe has is Luke, when it should have been Troy, but I know my husband would be happy that Joe has the next best thing.

Troy and Luke were like brothers.

Luke crouches down just in time to catch the bundle of toddler energy that flies towards him.

"Wuke!" Joe cries again with a laugh as he's scooped up into Luke's arms and carried back inside.

"Hey, bud. I missed you... I haven't seen you since yesterday." Luke ruffles Joe's hair. "Did you miss me too?"

Joe nods eagerly.

They melt my heart, the two of them – what's left of the fragmented pieces anyway.

"Joe, honey, can you tell Luke he doesn't need to knock on the door please? He won't listen to me," I tease as I shut the door.

"Wock, wock, who dere?" Joe replies animatedly.

Luke chuckles, that deep, manly laugh of his as he sets Joe down to the ground.

He drops his big body to the floor, and Joe parks his bottom right next to him, shuffling in as he tries to get even closer.

It's like I don't even exist in my child's eyes when Luke's here. My son craves male one-on-one time and Luke seems more than willing to fulfil that obligation.

I lean against the door frame and watch the two of them making 'vroom vroom' noises with toy cars and laughing together gleefully.

My heart is so full in this moment, that I instantly feel guilty for not missing Troy.

I do my best to push the feeling back down deep. This feeling of contentment isn't for me – it's for Joe. He's the one with a full life.

He doesn't even know that he's missing out on anything, and if that's the only thing I can give him as a parent, then I'll be happy.

***

I glance over at the handsome man sitting at my kitchen table.

Joe has been down for about half an hour, after two bed time stories and three cuddles from Luke, so now it's just the two of us.

I've known Luke for a long time now, but there are still so many things about him that I don't understand at all.

One of which is why he's here when he could be out having a life. A real life where he meets people and has adventures. A life where I'm not holding him back.

"What?" he asks me curiously as I stare at him.

He's gorgeous, he really is, and he's kind, sweet and genuine... any woman would be mad not to snap him up.

"Why don't you date? I've seen the way those single mums eye you up when you mow the lawns at school. You've been back two years and I don't think I've ever seen you with a woman."

He shrugs and takes a sip of the one and only beer he'll drink tonight. "I guess I'm not really interested."

I resist the urge to roll my eyes. "Why not?"

He's a heterosexual male. Of *course* he's interested in women.

I want him to find someone to share his life with, I *do*, but I'm not stupid enough to think that we could still have him the same way if he were to get married and have his own children.

I'm not sure I'm ready to give him up just yet. I might *never* be if I'm being honest.

I know Joe certainly isn't willing to let him go.

He sits down his bottle and gives me a look that makes me feel uncomfortable. It's got an edge of intensity to it that I'm not accustomed to seeing in his eyes. It's like he's seeing me – really seeing me.

"I've got everything I need already," he answers simply.

I shuffle my weight from foot to foot. I feel off kilter and I don't know why. Luke is the only person I feel one hundred percent comfortable with these days.

I laugh nervously. "You don't want to be alone forever, Luke."

He leans forward and rests his elbows on the table. "Neither do you, Mia."

I restlessly wring the tea towel I'm holding in my hands.

I'm stuck for words. There's something in the air I can't place. He's looking at me differently than he normally does.

"And besides..." he says after a few beats of awkward silence. "I'm not alone, I've got you and Joe."

I can feel the thumping of my heart in my chest, but I have no idea why the rate of it is increasing.

This is Luke.

Sure, he's gorgeous, smart, funny and kind. But he's *Luke*. *My Luke.*

The thought crosses my mind and it's not until it has that I realise I *do* think of him as mine. I've claimed him these past two years, but not in the way he deserves a woman to.

He deserves so much more than being babysitter to his best friend's widow and their son. He deserves real love and someone to share his life with.

I know I should step back from his life, and let him free to live it, but I can't seem to make my mouth say the words.

Instead, I duck my gaze and quietly reply. "And we've got you too."

I hear him push his chair out and get to his feet.

"You wash, I'll dry," he says, taking the towel from my hands.

I peek up at him and he's back to the Luke I know. I breathe out a breath of relief and nod at him.

I scrub the dishes and hand them to him in silence. We work alongside each other like an old married couple.

"What are you doing this weekend?" he asks when we're nearly done.

I huff out a breath and brace myself for what I've been avoiding telling him. "I forgot to tell you... Robert and Everly are coming to visit."

He groans. "Did you tell them to book a hotel this time?"

I scrunch up my nose and shake my head at him.

"*Mia*," he moans. "You can't keep doing this to yourself."

"I know. But I couldn't say no. You know how they are."

"I know exactly how they are, and that's why I don't want them coming in here and upsetting you."

"It's only two nights this time," I reply quietly. Not that that'll make a difference. Two nights with Troy's parents is two nights too many as far as I'm concerned.

I'm such a complete sucker.

I know they've been through a lot – no parent should have to bury their child – but it's no excuse for the way they behave towards me now, over two years on.

I don't know what goes through Everly's head, but whatever it is, it's not pleasant.

She seems to resent me for being here when her son isn't. It's messed up.

Every visit from the two of them results in me crying on Luke's shoulder long after they've gone, so I understand his frustration at my weakness. It can't be easy for him to pick up the pieces, over and over again.

I just don't know how to tell my in-laws that they're not welcome in their own son's house.

"When do they arrive?"

"Saturday morning."

"I'll come over to act as a buffer," he says with a sigh.

I'm so grateful for his offer. I know he's about as fond of the two of them as I am – perhaps even less. Where they seem to resent me, they appear to blame Luke for their son's death.

I know I should say no, tell him that I'll be fine – but I know I won't. Every minute that he's here is a minute I don't have to spend alone with the ice queen and her loyal lap dog. But even if they weren't totally awful, I'm not sure I'd ever turn down more time with Luke.

"Thank you," I whisper.

"Anytime, Mia," he replies.

CHAPTER FOUR

Luke

I wake to the sound of my phone ringing loudly.

I reach blindly for my cell and swipe at the screen to answer it.

"Hello?" I say groggily. The ringing doesn't stop. I look at the screen of the phone. That's because *this* is not what's ringing.

I scrub at my face and flick on the light.

It's my landline ringing.

I glance at the clock. It's two in the freaking morning.

I blink against the harsh light in confusion.

No one calls me on my landline.

No one except Mia.

I reach for the phone at lightning speed. I'm suddenly wide awake and filled with fear.

"Mia?" I answer even though I've got no proof it's her – I just *know*.

"Luke, it's *me*," she replies in a hushed tone.

She's scared – terrified even. I can tell just from those three words.

"What is it, sweetheart?" My words come out in a panicked rush.

I reach for my jeans and start pulling them on. I can't explain it, but I know she needs me – urgently.

Ice slides through my veins as she replies in a whisper. "I think there's someone trying to get into the house."

"Have you got your cell?" I demand.

"I'm on it now."

"Can you get to Joe?"

"I'm already in his room," she whispers.

"Push his dresser in front of the door and don't open it until you hear my voice, you got it, Mia?"

"Okay," she whispers, and I can hear the tremble in her voice.

"Do it now, Mia, okay? I'm coming, sweetheart. I'll be right there."

I'm already halfway out the door – my portable land line still in my hand.

"The phone is going to cut off, okay, I've got my cell."

"*Luke,*" she pleads, and it damn near breaks my heart.

"I'm comin–"

The line goes dead, and I slam the door shut on my truck and back down the drive faster than I ever have before.

Mia only lives a block and a half away, but right now it seems like too far.

If something happens to her or Joe, I'll never forgive myself.

I fly down the street, ignoring every speed and road rule as I do.

I stop a few houses down from Mia's and slip out the door, closing it as quietly as I can behind me. If there's someone there, the last thing I want is for them to get away.

Whoever it is, they're going to pay for messing with the wrong woman – *my* woman.

Because she's mine to protect now, and I know damn well that I'd kill for Mia Vander if I had to.

I creep down the street in the darkness, my ears on high alert for anything out of place.

The front of the house is clear, but I'm not surprised; if I was going to break into a place, I sure as shit wouldn't go in through the front.

I stick to the fence line, lurking in the shadows.

I nearly reach the back of the house when I hear the noise that must have woken Mia. It's an awful noise, the sound of metal rubbing against metal.

I peek around the side of the house.

I can't make out anything other than the shape of two bodies in the moonlight.

They're murmuring to one another, but I can't hear what they're saying. They aren't big guys – at a guess I'd say they were only young men, maybe even teenagers.

"Got it," I think I hear one of them say.

Not today, Satan.

I take a deep breath and I'm about to charge in there like a bull in a china shop when my phone rings, loud and shrill from my pocket.

It's Mia. I know that already. She's panicking.

"Run!" one of the assholes yells to the other.

I fly around the side of the house, my phone still ringing.

I can see where they're heading, over the back fence.

I'm chasing after them, when the loud ringing reminds me of the terrified woman in the house who needs me far more than I need to satisfy my urge of beating the shit out of those guys.

I stop in my tracks and I pull my phone out, which has stopped ringing now, and dial for the police – I give them the essential details and hang up.

These lowlifes have got the window wide open back here and for all I know, there wasn't just the two of them – there could be someone inside too.

I unlock the back door with my key and slip inside the house, doing my best to be quiet.

I creep through the hallway, checking each room as I go.

I can't hear or see anything at all out of place.

I've nearly decided that it's all clear when I hear the sound of feet on the staircase.

I push forward in the darkness, Mia and Joe are up there, and I'll be cold and dead before I let something happen to either of them.

I linger at the bottom, hiding in the shadows. Whoever I can hear, they're coming down.

I crouch low to the ground, ready to hurl myself at the invader.

They reach the bottom of the stairs and just stand there, unmoving.

I leap out and grab the person from behind, pinning their hands to their sides.

I was right. These are nothing but kids. This dude is tiny.

A loud sob rips through the air at the same time as the familiar smell wafts past my nose.

"*Mia?*" I whisper.

"Oh my god, *Luke*," she chokes out.

I can feel her heart hammering against my chest.

"What the hell are you doing down here, Mia? For Christ's sake, I could have hurt you. I told you to stay put."

She's still in my arms, pinned against me. Her back to my front.

"I heard your phone ringing outside... I knew you'd keep me safe," she replies quickly.

"Fucking hell, Mia," I growl.

The mere thought of her putting herself in harm's way has my blood boiling.

"You're squeezing me," she whispers.

I know I am, but I need her close. Safe.

I reluctantly release her and feel around for the light switch on the wall.

The light comes on in the living room, throwing a soft glow out into the hallway and onto us.

I look her up and down, looking for any sign that she's hurt.

I find no sign of injury, instead what I see is the sexiest sight I've ever laid eyes on.

She's wearing this tiny pair of white boy-short underwear, and a tight black singlet top – no bra.

Her hair is all wild and unruly and her cheeks are flushed.

"*Jesus*, Mia," I say, and this time it has nothing to do with her putting herself in danger.

My eyes rake greedily over her body and there's nothing I can do to stop myself.

"Where's Joe?" I choke out.

The only thing on my mind other than her tight little body, is her son, who I need to know is safe and well.

"He's in bed. He's fine. He didn't even wake," she reassures me.

"Wait here," I demand as I reluctantly pull my eyes from her. "I mean it this time, Mia. *Stay. Here.*"

She nods quickly, her head making short, jerky motions.

I rush up the stairs and check every room, seeing for myself that Joe is in fact still sleeping soundly, before going back to the staircase.

She's standing exactly where I left her at the bottom.

"It's all clear," I tell her.

She nods again. "Someone was here though, weren't they?" There's a tremble in her voice again that hurts me.

I hate seeing her scared.

I walk down the stairs until I'm standing right in front of her.

I nod. I could lie to make her feel safer, but I wouldn't do that. I could never lie to Mia.

"I saw two. My phone rang, and they got spooked."

Her eyes are as wide as saucers and I see the exact moment that she freaks out.

She sways, but I catch her before she can fall. I'll always be there to catch her before she falls.

"Shhhh," I tell her as I tug her against my body. "It's okay, I'm here, you're safe. Joe is fine."

Her hands snake around my waist and fist my shirt. "*Luke.*" She sobs.

"Shhhh."

I rub slow circles on her back and stroke her hair gently.

I feel her take a deep, steadying breath and I kiss the top of her blonde hair.

She sniffs, once, twice and then looks up at me, but doesn't let go.

"I'm sorry."

"There's nothing to be sorry for," I say, because it's true. There's nothing for her to apologise for.

"I can't keep using you like this, Luke."

"You're not *using* me," I reassure her.

There's a stray strand of hair that's found its way across her forehead, and I run my hand up her face and brush it off.

The movement is slow, sensual and deliberate.

I know I'm teetering on the edge of dangerous territory right now.

I've got a half-dressed Mia – the woman I've fallen head over heels in love with when I shouldn't have – in my arms, and I'm touching her face.

"You shouldn't have to keep saving me," she whispers.

Her voice sounds hoarse, and I let myself believe for a moment that maybe she feels this thing between us too. That it's not just all in my mind.

I run my thumb over her cheekbone, our eyes still locked in a heated standoff.

"I'd save you every single day for the rest of my life if you needed me to, Mia," I answer gruffly.

I tilt my head down, just a fraction, bringing our faces that tiny bit closer together.

I want to kiss her so badly it hurts, but I *can't*. She's my best friend's wife, and even though he's not here anymore, Mia doesn't feel that way about me.

I'm her protector, not her lover. I couldn't possibly be…

She runs her tongue along her bottom lip and breathes my name. "*Luke.*"

Her eyes are full of so much in this moment... fear, anxiousness, worry, maybe even desire...

"*Mia*," I reply as my thumb drags over her full lip.

She pushes up on her tip toes, slowly, her green eyes never leaving my blue ones.

She pauses for a moment before pressing her lips to mine.

I'm so shocked I just stand there as she kisses me.

It's the middle of the night and Mia is kissing *me*.

I feel like I'm in a dream – this can't really be happening.

A knock at the front door breaks the spell cast over us and Mia pulls away abruptly.

"Oh my god, I'm so sorry, I shouldn't have—"

"*Don't*," I interrupt her. "Don't do that. Don't you dare apologise for that."

She's freaking out. I've gotten the closest to her that I ever have and she's trying to take it all back – I can't let that happen.

"But I *kissed* you," she whispers, her cheeks bright red and her eyes wide.

She lets go of my shirt and steps back against the wall like she can't get away fast enough.

"I should be the one apologising," I growl at her as I step forward so my body is flush against hers again. "Because I didn't kiss *you* first."

I don't give her a chance to argue again. My lips are on hers before she has time to think – time to decide that this is a bad idea.

Her hands grip my arms, and mine her jaw, as she gives in to the kiss entirely.

Our mouths move together like they've been doing it for years.

The knock at the door sounds again and I pull away reluctantly with a sigh against her lips.

"We'd better get that," she whispers.

I give her a chaste kiss on the lips.

"Go get some clothes on, it's probably the police."

"Mmm hmm," she murmurs.

I kiss her again.

"Clothes."

"Okay." She nods but doesn't make any move to go.

I kiss her once more and flex my self-control as I step away from her. We'll never answer the door at this rate.

"I'll get dressed," she says, as she steps backwards up the steps, her eyes still on mine.

God, she looks so beautiful like this.

"I'll get the door," I say, unmoving.

She lets out a nervous giggle and turns, rushing up the stairs.

"God damn," I mutter to myself as I head for the front door. "That was unexpected."

CHAPTER FIVE

Mia

I can still feel the burn in my cheeks as I shut the door behind the detective who has just spent the better part of an hour asking us a whole bunch of questions.

I felt like I had a big neon sign flashing over my head saying, 'I'm guilty – arrest me – I just kissed my late husband's best friend'.

Luke's still here – of course – he'd never leave me to deal with anything like this alone. He's such a good man.

And I kissed him.

I don't know what on earth went through my head, but it just felt right.

It's been so long since I've had a man pressed up against me like that, and it wasn't just *some man* either, it was a familiar one, one that feels like home, and I *kissed* him.

After everything he's done for Joe and me, I came onto him like some kind of desperate slag.

I don't know what to do now. Half of me wants to go upstairs and hide under my covers, and the other half wants to go into the living room and kiss him again.

I don't know if it's the adrenaline from tonight's events, or if it's something more, but I've never felt this way about Luke before now.

Sure, I've noticed how good looking he is – I'm widowed, not blind – but I've never thought about a man other than Troy in this way until now, and it's scaring me.

I cover my face with my hands.

Troy.

I've just betrayed Troy... with his closest friend of all people. I don't really want to think about what kind of person that makes me.

"Mia?" I hear Luke's raspy voice say my name.

I peek from between my fingers.

"Don't beat yourself up."

He's leaning his hip against the door frame of the living room, watching me carefully.

He's reading my mind, again. Knowing exactly how I'm feeling seems to be a talent of his.

"But what about Troy?" I whisper. "What have we done?"

The words hang in the air between us as my hands drop to my side.

"I don't know." He shrugs, but I can see the conflict in his eyes.

I'd be willing to bet it mirrors my own.

"I shouldn't have kissed you."

"It's a bit late for shouldn'ts," he says with a sigh.

"Can we just pretend it never happened?" I ask him hopefully.

He watches me so carefully I can feel it all the way deep in my bones.

I feel him all over – the way his lips touched mine... there's no way I'm going to forget that kiss anytime soon – I'm not even fooling myself with my ridiculous request.

"If that's what you want, Mia, then it's forgotten."

He's such a good man. I could ask him for anything in the world and he'd make it happen. He'd go to the ends of the earth to take care of me and Joe.

I nod yes, even though everything inside of me tells me I should say no, that it's not what I really want, but I don't. "Thank you," I say instead.

"*Anything* for you, Mia."

He's looking at me with those intense eyes again and it's too much. *He's* too much. The way my name sounds coming from his lips makes me shiver.

"I better get back to bed, Joe will be up in a few hours…"

I walk towards the stairs, but he makes no move to leave. He will soon though, he'll leave, and I'll be here, alone and vulnerable again.

"Luke?" I turn back so I can look at him. I shouldn't ask him for anything more, but I will anyway, I need him too much. "Would you stay the rest of the night? I don't want to be alone."

He smiles and shakes his head at me. "Did you really think I was going to leave you here by yourself?"

I shrug as relief floods through me.

"I'll be on the couch, Mia. I'll see you when you wake up, okay? You can relax, I'll keep you and Joe safe."

I know he will. He always has.

I take a couple of steps up the staircase before stopping again.

"Hey, Luke?" I call down to him.

He's still standing in the same spot, watching me like a hawk.

He raises his brows.

"I never said thank you – for coming to our rescue."

"It was nothing, Mia."

I wouldn't call running around in the dark and scaring off thieves or predators, *nothing*, but I can see he's not going to change his mind.

"Well thank you anyway. I don't know what I'd do without you," I tell him.

I turn back and start up the stairs again.

"I hope you never have to find out," I hear him whisper.

I rush up the final step and into the safety of my bedroom.

I take a big, deep breath and try to figure out what the hell just happened.

CHAPTER SIX

Luke

I stretch my back out and lift my arms up over my head.

That couch in Mia's living room isn't made for a man my size, no matter how much I try to convince her that it's fine.

I could sleep in the spare room, like Mia keeps suggesting, but I know she's still nervous, so downstairs is where she needs me to be – even if she won't admit it.

"Bad back, old man?" Caleb jokes.

I flip him the middle finger and he grins. He looks so much like Troy when he smiles like that.

They've got the same jet black hair and bright green eyes too.

Caleb's smaller than Troy was, but they still look more similar than what is easy to look at. I don't know how Caleb could even look in the mirror without seeing his brother staring back at him.

"I've been sleeping on Mia's couch all week," I grumble.

He frowns. "She still spooked?"

I nod. The woman is as nervous as a bag of cats at a greyhound meet.

"That sucks... I bet Joe is loving it though."

"You'd think it was Christmas every morning." I chuckle.

"How is my nephew? I haven't seen him in a week or so."

"He's good. You should call in, just maybe do it sooner rather than later, your folks are due in town tomorrow morning."

I brace myself for the string of curses that are bound to fly out of his mouth, and sure enough, he doesn't disappoint.

"Where'd you learn all those words?" I chuckle deeply.

He ignores me. "What the fuck are they coming to town for?"

"To make Mia's life hell, what do you think?" I shrug.

"Sounds about right," he sneers.

Caleb hasn't spoken to his parents for about a year now.

One day he just snapped. Didn't need that kind of negativity in his life he said.

I couldn't blame the kid.

It might sound harsh to just cut off your parents, especially after their son – your brother – died, but Robert and Everly aren't acting like parents anymore. They're acting like spoiled, hurtful, little children, and Caleb doesn't deserve that.

"They're disguising it as a visit to see Joe, of course," I huff as I dig.

Caleb drives his shovel into the hard ground with a little more force than necessary.

"She needs to cut them off. Her and Joe don't need to put up with their shit."

"You're preaching to the choir, man," I tell him. "I've been on her to tell them to get a hotel for a year. She's too scared."

"Maybe I'll go over there this weekend."

I chuckle. "Oh no you don't, that's not going to help Mia or Joe."

"Well we can't just let them treat her like crap like every other time."

I drive my shovel into the ground and leave it sitting there. I wipe the sweat off my brow with the back of my arm. "Don't worry, I've got this."

"Yeah?" he asks as he stops his digging too.

I nod. "I know Mia doesn't want a fuss, but I'm not picking up the pieces again, I can't watch Mia break down like that anymore. If they're there, then so am I."

"You're a good guy, Luke. My brother was lucky to have you on his side. Mia and Joe don't know how good they've got it."

I swallow the lump in my throat and don't reply.

I bet he wouldn't be saying that if he knew what had happened on Tuesday night between his sister-in-law and myself.

The way she pressed her lips to mine... the way she tasted on my tongue...

I need to stop thinking about it – Mia seems to want to move on, and I need to as well.

I've stayed there every night since and she's not touched me once – actually forget touched, she's not even come within an arm's length of me.

She's avoided eye contact too, and if she thinks she's doing a good job of forgetting that anything happened between us, then she better think again.

Anyone who knows us even a little bit would know that something was up the minute they set foot in the room.

In fact, if my sister Emily were to call in, we'd be totally and utterly screwed.

She'd open Pandora's box within seconds.

I make a mental note to tell her that the Vanders will be visiting this weekend – that ought to buy us some time to get back to normal.

I let my mind wander back to the moment when Mia looked at me with want in her eyes.

I don't want to go back to normal, but I know I have to.

I shouldn't even be thinking about Mia at all, let alone thinking about wanting *more* of her.

Troy would be turning in his grave.

I glance back at Caleb, who's getting stuck into digging again, and try to focus on the job we've got to get done, rather than every which way I'd like to kiss Mia.

***

"Wuke sleep dere?" Joe points to the couch.

He's all washed up and in his pyjamas, ready for bed.

"Yeah, buddy, I'll sleep here again, I'll be here to see you in the morning."

He claps his hands together and giggles gleefully.

"Say goodnight to Luke, baby, I'll take you up for a story."

He comes over to me, his arms wide and wraps them around my neck.

"Nigh nigh, Wuke," he says as he squeezes me.

"Night, little guy," I reply as I hug him back.

He lets go of me and runs over to take Mia's out-stretched hand.

"Wuv you, Wuke," he calls back over his shoulder.

My head snaps up and I meet Mia's surprised eyes. He's never told me he loves me before.

My heart swells in my chest. I love that little boy like he's my very own. He might be a little mini version of his father, but he's my boy in a lot of ways. I'm the main male figure in his life.

Mia and I are still staring at each other in disbelief.

Joe stops short of the bottom of the stairs. "Wuv you, Wuke," he says again. He stares at me like he's waiting for a response.

I clear my throat, which is thick with emotion.

"I ah... I love you too, bud," I choke out.

He grins at me and waves before pulling Mia off up the stairs.

I might be head over heels in love with his mumma, but that kid has just well and truly stolen my heart.

***

"You wanna watch a movie with me, Mia?"

I can hear her mucking around out in the kitchen. I know she's stalling for time. Everything is tidy in there, has been for ages, she's just scared to be alone with me.

"Ummm, what are you thinking of watching?" she calls back.

She appears in the doorway, her face a nervous mask.

I shrug. "Whatever you want."

"I was thinking I might just go get an early night..."

I glance at my watch. "It's seven-thirty, Mia. It's too early for an early night."

She shoots me a sheepish grimace.

"Sit down with me, sweetheart, I promise I won't bite." I pat the spot on the couch next to me.

"*Biting* is not what I'm afraid of," she mutters under her breath.

I hold back a smile and pretend I didn't hear her.

"What do you want to watch?" I ask as I flick through the channels.

She sits down on the couch, as far away from me as she possibly can, tucking her legs underneath her as she does.

"There's some romantic chick flick on?" I offer.

"No," she answers quickly. "No romance."

No romance. Alright then. Hint taken.

"What about a comedy?"

"Are there any thrillers on?"

I bite back a laugh. I see what she's doing here. She doesn't want to get too comfortable with me. She's trying her best to keep her guard up.

"I think this one is?"

I point with the remote at the screen and glance at her.

She nods eagerly.

I do my best not to grin. "Alright then."

I sit my feet up on the coffee table and throw my arms over the back of the couch.

I can see Mia's plan here, I really can, but I already know it's going to fail. She's a total chicken shit. If she stays over there all alone until the end of this movie, I'll eat my hat.

It only takes half an hour for me to realise I'm one hundred percent on target with my assumption.

Mia is halfway across the couch already, clutching a pillow like it would be able to protect her in some way.

I haven't got much of a clue about what's going on with the storyline, but I don't care.

Listening to her little gasps and watching her reactions is far more interesting to me than any movie.

"Oh no, *don't* go in there," she hisses at the screen.

I chuckle quietly.

She shuffles closer to me again.

"Oh no, no, no..." she half hides behind her pillow shield. "You stupid girl..."

I laugh louder. "Come here, Mia."

I lift my arm, indicating that she should come and sit against my side.

She doesn't hesitate; in fact she almost throws herself over at me.

She snuggles into my side and I let my arm drape over her back protectively.

I like the fact that she finds safety with me – even if it is just from a scary movie.

She buries her face into my chest and waits.

"She went in there," I drawl as I look back at the screen.

"Of course she did. They always do," she squeaks as she peeks back out at the TV.

She jumps as the killer attacks the woman in question.

"Why'd you make me watch this?" she groans. "I'll have nightmares for a week."

"Hey, don't blame me, I wanted to watch the chick flick, remember?" I chuckle.

She looks away from the screen and up at me.

I don't think she even knows she's done it, but her arms are wrapped around my middle tightly like she's holding on for dear life.

She rests her chin on my chest and just sits there, looking like a beautiful, sweet angel.

"You're making a bit of a habit of coming to my rescue." She pouts.

I chuckle and reach for her hair, so I can play with the blonde strands.

"You make it too easy, Mia."

"I think I've made myself entirely too easy," she mumbles as she drops her gaze.

I grip her chin between my fingers and force her to look at me. "Don't you dare talk about yourself like that," I demand in a tone that leaves no room for bullshit. "You might regret what happened between us the other night, and that's fine, but don't you think about yourself like that ever again."

Her eyes widen in surprise, but I don't care. I might rarely speak to Mia in anything other than a soothing tone, but I won't stand for her putting herself down.

Certainly not because of something that I'm to blame for.

"You got it?" I press.

"Okay," she replies quietly.

We stare at each other for a long, long moment. I don't know about her, but I'm thinking things I know I shouldn't... I can't seem to stop.

She's just so breathtaking.

She has no idea of the power she holds over me.

She thinks I'm here out of obligation, and in the beginning, I was. But now I'm here because there's nowhere else I'd rather be.

"I can't stop thinking about it," she whispers.

I know she can't. I watched her mind ticking over all week.

She's still beating herself up about betraying Troy.

"He was like a brother to me, Mia, I don't want to betray his memory any more than you do."

"That's not what I'm talking about." She blushes a soft pink.

I twist her hair around my finger as I watch her.

"Then what?"

Her eyes widen slightly. "I can't stop thinking about *it*."

"I think you're going to have to spell it out for me, Mia."

"I can't get how much I liked kissing *you* out of my head," she admits.

I'm surprised, shocked even. I really thought she regretted it.

I can't stop thinking about how much I liked it either and I need to tell her that. This is it. This is my moment and I have to make it count.

"Neither can I, Mia, I can't think of anything else."

"You can't?" she asks. I can hear insecurity in her voice and I don't like it.

I twist my body, just a fraction so our chests are touching.

"I've wanted to kiss you like that for six months, sweetheart."

Genuine surprise is written all over her face. She really had no idea of my growing infatuation.

"I want to do it again right now," I admit.

"You didn't say anything..." she whispers.

"Falling in love with your best mate's wife isn't exactly something you want to scream from the roof tops."

Her jaw drops, and I realise exactly what I've just said.

"*Luke...*"

"*Shit*," I mutter. "I'm sorry, Mia, it just came out without thinking. I'm sorry."

"You're in love with me?"

I could lie to her, but it's not a real option for me. I'm not willing to lie to Mia any more now than I was yesterday – even if I risk losing her by telling the truth.

"If it's not love, it's a lot like it," I reply honestly.

"But... but... you're my best friend, Luke."

"You're my best friend too," I tell her, and I mean it. Troy was like a part of me, but these past two years, the only person I really want to spend time with is the woman in front of me – and her little boy. "Joe is too."

"I can't lose you." Her eyes well with tears.

"You are never going to lose me, Mia. I promise you, okay?"

"You don't know that." Her bottom lip wobbles.

I know that Troy promised her that she'd never have to be without him either, and now he's gone. But this is different. This isn't a battle zone – not until her in-laws turn up at least – I'm not going to get killed by a stray bullet or grenade.

"Well I'll promise you this then; I'll never walk away from you willingly. I'll never leave you on purpose, Mia. No matter how you feel about me or how I feel about you. I'll be here until you tell me to leave."

She nods and sniffs back her tears.

"I'm not expecting you to love me back, sweetheart, okay? I know you're not there, and that's fine... I don't want to make things weird between us, but I guess that's kind of shot to hell after the other night anyway."

"I just had no idea..." She shakes her head in obvious disbelief.

"I know." I nod.

"Would you have told me if the other night hadn't happened?"

I shake my head. "No. I know you've got enough on your plate."

"I'm glad I know," she whispers.

"You are?"

"Mmm hmm." She nods. She's quiet for a long while before she speaks again. "You know how you said you wanted to kiss me again?"

I nod slowly, not knowing where she's going with this.

"I might not be able to say I'm in love with you, Luke, but I want you to kiss me again so badly I can't think of anything else."

I cup her cheek in my rough hand and lean down until our noses are touching.

"You're all I can think about, Mia... when I fall asleep at night and when I wake up in the morning."

She sighs, a sweet breathy sound, before our lips meet.

I intended to kiss her softly, sweetly, but it seems that Mia has other ideas.

Her tongue runs along my bottom lip, and it must make me the worst man in the world, because here I am, in my best friend's living room, kissing his wife like she's mine and not giving a shit about the consequences.

Not even a flash of Troy's smiling face in my mind is enough to keep me from opening my mouth and slipping my tongue into Mia's mouth.

She tastes like heaven and smells like home.

"Mia," I groan.

"*Luke*," she murmurs against my lips. I know it's not the name she wishes she were saying, but it's good enough for me.

Before I even know what's happening, she's clambering into my lap, so she's straddling me.

I groan and kiss her deeply.

She's got me so hard, I bet she can feel it through my jeans.

This isn't the way I want things to go with Mia, but if she tries to take it further, I doubt I'll have the will power to say no.

I know I should stop it now, in case it does go too far, but I *can't* – this is every fantasy I've had for the past few months come to life.

I want Mia Vander – I want her in any way I can have her, no matter how inappropriate it might be.

Thankfully, she chooses that moment to pull back, before my self-control evacuates the building entirely. She's breathing so heavy and her eyes are alight with excitement.

She leans in so our foreheads are resting against one another as my hands rub up and down from her waist to her hips.

"You could have any woman you want, you know that, right?"

I don't know that at all, but it still wouldn't make a scrap of difference to me.

"The only woman I'm interested in, is you, Mia."

I watch the blush slowly creep onto her cheeks as she smiles and bites down on her lip.

"I know I shouldn't like the sound of that, but I do."

I chuckle. "At least you're honest."

She sighs and sits back. "What do we do now, Luke?"

"Nothing," I say simply. "We do whatever feels right, and nothing else."

She nods. "I like the sound of that."

I absolutely love the sound of that, but I think I've said enough for one night, so instead I just reach for her neck and pull her mouth back to mine.

CHAPTER SEVEN

Mia

I run my finger over my lips for the hundredth time as I finish up in the bathroom. I can still feel the blush of my cheeks and it heats more as I think about the mental image of me sitting in Luke's lap.

I can feel him everywhere – his touch on my skin, his mouth on mine, the feel of his breath on my face… the tingling feeling of my spine when his eyes find mine.

He's waking emotions inside of me that I thought were dead and buried with my husband.

I know it's wrong, but I can't stop the way I feel.

Troy was always big on that. He always said that it didn't matter what anyone else thought, what mattered was how you felt.

And now here I am, in a predicament I never thought I'd find myself in.

Luke is falling in love with *me*.

I don't know what to make of that. I didn't think another man would ever see me the way he obviously does.

The only man I've ever been *in* love with is Troy.

I don't know how to fall in love again – I'm not sure it's even possible.

I glance over at the photo from our wedding that still sits next to my side of the bed.

MR. MARCH   45

Just a picture of him is enough to make me catch my breath.

I'm still madly in love with a man that's not here anymore. I've tried, but I can't get over him.

It's not like when you have a break up and you go your separate ways, this isn't like that at all. It's the person you love more than anything being there one minute and gone the next.

I know it's been more than two years since I've seen his face or heard his voice, but I still love him as much now as I did then.

I can still picture his smile and hear his laugh in my head.

I can imagine the way he used to kiss me and hold my hand.

Troy was my first boyfriend, first kiss, first *everything*...

But now it's not just him. It's him *and* Luke.

I picture myself kissing and I don't know who I'm kissing anymore. The image merges from Troy to Luke and back again and that scares me.

My memories are all I have left of my husband now, and I don't know how I feel about possibly losing them by letting myself get caught up in another man.

I climb under the covers and reach for the frame, bringing it to my chest.

"I'm sorry, Troy."

I miss him so much. I don't know how I'm getting through life without him.

Luke. My brain tells me. *He's getting you through.*

I shut out the thoughts – even though I know they're on the money.

I can't turn off the feelings I'm having for Luke, and truthfully, I don't want to, but I don't know how to do this... I don't know how to let Luke in without pushing Troy out.

I look down at the picture one last time before closing my eyes.

I'll worry about it tomorrow. For now, just for tonight, I let myself believe that I won't be alone forever, and let my dreams decide exactly what that means for my heart.

***

"Luke, can you please just carry that trash out to the end of the drive? And then you can take off if you want to..."

I don't want him to go. The last thing I want is to be alone when the monster-in-laws arrive, but I can't expect him to stay. He's been my personal bodyguard all week, and the man looks shattered.

He's entirely too big to sleep on my couch, but there's no telling him.

He's loyal and protective to a fault.

This is his weekend too, and I know he won't want to spend it with two people that are so utterly horrible, but I'd still be willing to bet all the money I've got on him staying put.

"I'll take it out now, but I'm not going anywhere, Mia, you know that."

I don't bother arguing. He won't change his mind, and I don't want him to anyway if I'm being honest with myself.

I scoop up Joe as he tries to follow after Luke. "Alright, baby, Nan and Pop will be here soon, okay? How exciting is that?"

"Pop," he repeats with a toothy grin.

The kid's smart. Robert is by far the lesser of the two evils when it comes to his grandparents.

"Why don't you go and find your new red truck to show him?"

He nods eagerly and squirms to be put down.

I watch him with a grateful smile. There's no way I could deal with these visits if it weren't for him.

Luke comes back inside and follows my line of sight to Joe. He smiles at him with so much love in his eyes it makes my heart feel like it could burst.

I should probably feel as confused about this as I do about kissing Luke, but it's hard.

I'm torn between Troy and Luke because I'm feeling the same things for both men. It's different with the role of being Joe's dad. I know Luke isn't Joe's father, but he's the closest thing to it at the moment.

I never got to see Troy as a dad. Our son was born six days after he passed away, so there's nothing to compare here. I don't feel guilty for letting Joe have this time with Luke – I feel guilty for sometimes feeling like there's nothing missing, but those moments are so fleeting I try not to let it get to me.

We're just doing the best we can, Luke, Joe and me.

I hear a car pull into the drive and I physically shudder.

Luke must have been watching me because he's at my side within seconds. "I've got your back, Mia, it'll be okay this time, I promise."

I know I shouldn't do it – not with the in-laws from hell about to walk through the front door, but I'm just so grateful for his support – with everything, that I press up on my tip toes and kiss him softly on the corner of his mouth.

He smiles so sweetly it makes my heart skip a beat. I've always liked his smile, but I've never noticed that he smiles at different people in different ways.

Among them all, he's got a Joe smile and another smile just for me.

I think that one might be my favourite out of all of them.

I can hear them coming up the path now, probably muttering about having to carry their own luggage and I brace myself as I plaster a fake smile on my face.

"Twuck," Joe announces as he barrels across the room to Luke.

Luke lifts him up and holds him in one arm, while his other arm rests on my lower back, gently guiding me forward.

There's a loud knock at the door, followed closely by another impatient one, and I have to work really hard to keep my lips turned up into a smile.

"Breathe, Mia," Luke tells me quietly as he opens the door.

Everly looks the same as always – like she's just sucked on a lemon, and Robert looks tired – I guess having a total bitch for a wife would do that to you.

I was wrong about them carrying their own luggage; it's still sitting in a pile next to the car.

"Everly, Robert, how are you?" I ask as sweetly as I can manage.

My welcome is met with a top-to-toe appraisal, which then follows up Luke's arm to his face.

"Mia... *Luke*," Everly replies curtly. "How interesting that *you* are here."

Luke's face twists into a scowl. "I'm here for Mia and Joe."

"Twuck," Joe announces and it's only then that either of his grandparents seem to notice his existence.

"Oh, hello my dear boy," Everly coos, transforming in an instant. "Come to Nan."

Joe screws up his nose as she reaches for him with her witches claws and turns to bury his face into Luke's arm.

Luke takes a deliberate step back and I want to hug him for saving Joe from that evil woman.

"Why don't you both come in," Luke suggests. "Mia was just going to make a cup of tea."

Everly mumbles something under her breath that I don't catch, and reluctantly steps inside the house.

I move to head for the kitchen, but Luke catches my hand and pulls me back. "I'll go get the royals' bags, you serve some food, okay? They can't complain if their mouths are full," he whispers in my ear.

A giggle slips out of my mouth and Luke grins at me wickedly.

I can see Everly glaring at me out of the corner of my eye and it makes my skin crawl. I can't figure out why I'm so afraid of this woman, but there's something stopping me from telling her how I really feel.

Joe reaches for me and I take him into my arms and carry him into the kitchen.

I hear Luke and Robert say their hellos, but I don't look back. The wicked witch of the west is hot on my heels and if I stop moving, she just might eat me alive.

I sit Joe in his chair to save him from having to be passed around and flick the jug on to boil the water.

"So, did you have a nice trip down?" I finally ask when I can't stall any longer.

I turn around and find Everly sitting at the dining table next to Joe – who looks less than comfortable – and Robert looking at some photos of Troy on the living room wall.

"It was bearable," Everly replies, speaking for the first time directly to me.

"What about you, Robert? How's work going?"

"Oh, you know," he answers with a smile. "Same thing different day."

I actually quite like Robert, but the man has absolutely no balls, and in my opinion, standing back and watching a bully carry on without saying anything, is just as bad as being the bully.

He sees the way Everly talks to me and never says a word to her about it.

He walks over to the table and ruffles Joe's hair.

"Hey, boy. Whatcha got there?"

"Twuck," Joe announces proudly as he holds the truck up to show him.

I hear Luke come back through the front door, his arms full of bags and I mouth the word 'sorry' to him.

He winks at me and heads off up the stairs.

Everly looks around the kitchen and sniffs in a snooty way. "The décor is looking a little tired in here, darling, it could use a freshen up. You know Troy would never have let the place get run down."

I grind my teeth together to stop the retort on the end of my tongue.

I know she's trying to wind me up, and I can't let her succeed.

She's only been here five minutes.

"Can I get you a tea?" I ask instead.

"You know how I have it," she replies, her eyes never leaving Joe and her husband as they zoom the truck back and forth on the table.

There's no please, no thank you. Not even a bloody yes.

I inhale a deep breath and blow it out slowly as I get to work on making the queen her drink.

"Tea or coffee, Robert?" I ask without looking back.

"I'd love a coffee please," he replies.

I'm stirring the milk into one of the cups when I feel Luke come up behind me.

I don't have any doubt it's him – we're so used to one another at this point.

He hands me the dish for the used teabags without a word and screws the lid back on the milk once I'm done with it.

I put some biscuits out on a plate and hand out the tea and coffee before sitting down.

Luke sits next to me. He gives my leg a quick, reassuring squeeze under the table and I smile at him.

"Will you be joining us for dinner tonight, Luke?" Everly asks, but it's an accusation more than a question.

I haven't actually discussed what the sleeping arrangements will be tonight. I don't really need Luke here now that I have other company, but I still want it nonetheless.

I can't decide if I want him here more for safety or if it's purely because I don't like the idea of being away from him, and that scares me a bit.

Luke sits down his tea and meets her eyes. "I'm staying on the couch at the moment, ever since Mia had someone try to break in."

Everly clutches at her chest dramatically. "Oh, good heavens, did they get inside?"

I shake my head. "No, Luke took care of it."

"Well it's lucky that *Luke* was here then, wasn't it," she replies with attitude. "But Robert and I are here now, so your services won't be needed any longer."

Luke chuckles quietly, clearly unaffected by her. "I think I just might stick around. Mia will tell me if I've overstayed my welcome."

The idea is almost laughable. Luke could never overstay his welcome, not with me.

Everly makes a 'humph' noise before turning her back to the two of us and trying to talk to Joe.

I smile up at Luke. "Thank you," I mouth to him.

He taps the end of my nose with his finger. "Anytime, sweetheart," he whispers.

CHAPTER EIGHT

Luke

I'm a fairly patient man, but Christ, it's being tested right now.

If Troy's mother complains about the 'décor' in the house once more, I'm going to hand her a paint brush and tell her to get to fucking work.

There's nothing wrong with the house, but even if there was, it's none of her god damn business.

This isn't Troy's house anymore, it's Mia's, and having Everly roam around pointing out every little thing that Troy would have, or could have done is not helpful in the least.

If I didn't think it'd upset Mia, I would have yelled at her by now.

Troy's not coming back, and no amount of bitching and moaning is going to change the fact.

It's not even about Troy at this point.

Everly's just a horrible person and Robert is like a spineless jellyfish.

Mia deserves so much more than this shit.

I linger in the doorway of Joe's room as his so-called grandparents both say goodnight to him.

Everly rolls her eyes at me as she passes, and I send out a prayer that Mia can survive downstairs with the witch before I get back down there.

Robert is still sitting on the edge of Joe's bed, talking to him about the trains that he used to drive when he was younger.

Joe's eyes are wide and excited. He loves trains almost as much as trucks and dinosaurs.

"Domas?" he asks excitedly. "Domas?"

Robert looks over his shoulder at me in confusion.

"Thomas," I elaborate. "You know... 'Thomas the Tank Engine'."

"Oh of *course*," Robert replies, looking back at Joe with a grin. "You get some sleep and I'll show you some photos tomorrow. I think there was one in there that looked just like Thomas."

They say their goodnights and then it's just Joe and I.

He looks so cute cuddled up in his big-boy bed.

He's already so grown up it's scary.

"Your dad loved trains, buddy," I tell him as I sit down on the side of his bed. "Even got excited about them as an adult." I chuckle at an old memory.

"Twains," Joe mimics.

"Trains, trucks, cars... anything that went fast." I grin.

"Dad," he says.

I reach for the photo on his bedside table and turn it so he can see. It's a photo of Mia and Troy just before our last deployment.

"There's your mumma, and your dad." I point to the two of them.

"Mumma." He grins.

I look at the picture and smile. They were like night and day, Mia and Troy.

Mia is tiny, blonde and fair-skinned, Troy was huge, dark-haired and olive-skinned.

Joe is a mix of the two of them – fair-skinned and dark-haired. They both had green eyes, so it goes without saying that Joe was always going to inherit those.

"Dad." I point to Troy and show him again, but he doesn't seem interested anymore.

"Hug," he announces, holding his arms out wide for me to cuddle him.

I have to catch myself sometimes in moments like these. It's so bittersweet – receiving love and affection from Joe. I've been here to witness most of his firsts and I'm so thankful for that, but the sacrifice that led to me being the one here is not something I can take lightly.

"Goodnight, bud. I'll see you in the morning, okay?"

He nods and yawns as he untangles his arms from my neck and snuggles down into his pillow.

He's so sleepy already; it won't be long before he drifts off.

I sit and watch as his eyelids grow heavier and heavier until they're shut altogether. His lips form a little 'o' as sleep takes him deeper and deeper.

I've got so much love for this little guy – more than I thought I could have for another person. I care about Mia just as much, but this is different.

I can somewhat understand what people mean when they say that having a child is a different kind of love. He might not be my son, but he's such a big part of my life that I feel it anyway.

A hand on my shoulder startles me.

I look up and Mia is smiling down at me.

"Little stinker, I didn't even get to say goodnight," she whispers.

I kiss the hand that's sitting on my shoulder and she blushes. "He was worn out," I tell her.

"Aren't we all," she mumbles.

I take her other hand in mine and pull her until she's sitting in my lap.

"Is she still being a bitch?" I ask quietly.

"Does she ever stop?" Mia rolls her eyes. "She's grilling me about why you're here."

"You don't have to explain anything to her – to either of them, Mia."

"I know," she whispers. "She's just so horrible though, you know? She twists my words and makes me feel guilty for things that are outside of my control."

"This is the last time they're staying here, okay, sweetheart? I'm not having you put up with this again."

She wraps her arms around my shoulders and rests her head against mine.

"Thank you... for everything."

"I'd say it's a pleasure, but I don't want to start lying to you now," I say with a grin.

We're still whispering, even though Joe is well and truly out to it. Short of one of his beloved trains driving through the room, there's nothing that will wake him now.

"Well thank you for suffering for me." She giggles softly, and I feel the motion through my whole body.

I'd suffer forever if she asked me to, but I'm not going to tell her that. The last time I opened my mouth when she was in my arms, I said things I'd sworn I was going to keep to myself.

"We better get back down there before the bloodhound sniffs us out. The last thing we need is her seeing you in my lap."

Mia freezes and shudders. "Oh god, can you imagine?" She winces. "I'd never hear the end of it."

I kiss the top of her head.

"Two nights, sweetheart, just two nights and then they'll be gone."

***

I wake in the middle of the night with a searing pain in my back.

I can't stay on this god damn couch a minute longer.

I sit up and lean back against the arm of it.

I'm so uncomfortable I'm not sure I could fall back asleep down here if I tried, even though I'm exhausted.

Listening to someone nit-picking over you and the woman you love is draining as hell. I haven't ever had to stand up for someone the way I have for Mia this past evening.

I know Everly will be right back at it first thing in the morning, so I need to rest. My patience has worn as thin as it can go without snapping entirely.

I know I don't have many options right now.

I can't go to the spare room like I should have done in the beginning, because thing one and thing two are crashed out in there.

That only leaves me two choices.

Mia's room or home.

I know it's only one choice when it comes down to it.

I'd never abandon Mia and Joe in the middle of the night like this – not even with a note and a promise to return early.

I push up to my feet and roll out my shoulders.

Everything aches more now than it did after I'd spent a week digging holes.

I trudge up the stairs, feeling around for the railing rather than turning the lights on.

I can see a soft glow coming from under Mia's door – she sleeps with a small nightlight on near the door. I've never asked her why, but I assume it's because of losing Troy. Maybe that light makes her feel less alone.

I turn the handle quietly and push the door open, doing my best not to make any noise that might wake Joe down the hall.

I can make out Mia, huddled to one side of the big bed in the centre of the room.

It makes me sad that she still sleeps to one side, even after two years, but I guess old habits die hard.

"Mia," I whisper into the dim room.

I get no reply.

I creep closer to the bed. There's a fine line here between waking her gently and scaring the ever-loving shit out of her, and to be honest I'm not sure which side of that line I'm going to wind up on.

"Mia," I whisper slightly louder.

"Mmmm?" she murmurs, still pretty much asleep.

"Mia, it's Luke."

"*Luke.*" She sighs softly, sounding satisfied.

I can't stop myself from smiling at that.

"Mia, I'm going to sleep in here for a bit okay? My back is killing me."

MR. MARCH 59

She rolls over and lifts the blanket for me.

I'm not sure if she's even awake or not, but I'm not about to go back downstairs and put myself through another few hours of agony, so I round the bed and climb in next to her.

I rest my head on the pillow, facing her.

She looks so peaceful in her sleep, there's no stress or worry on her face.

"Goodnight, sweetheart," I whisper.

Her eyes blink sleepily as she shuffles her body closer to mine.

Her hand snakes out under the covers and her fingernails graze over my bare abdomen, causing me to shiver.

I should have put a shirt on. Me, lying next to Mia when I'm only half dressed, is not the best idea I've ever had. Sure, we've been sharing a few kisses here and there, but this is another step entirely.

She shuffles even closer, and on instinct, I lift my arm so she can tuck into my chest.

She might not be entirely conscious right now, but this is easily the best moment I've had in a long time.

She tilts her head back up to look at me as her fingers continue their travels over my skin.

"You have abs," she tells me, her voice thick with sleep.

I chuckle. "Yeah. I guess I do."

"There's so many of them..." she yawns.

I lean down and kiss her forehead. "Get some more sleep, Mia."

She sighs and wiggles around until she's comfortable, her head on my shoulder, her arm wrapped around my middle and her leg thrown over my leg.

Her skin feels entirely too good against mine, and if I was a better man, I'd get myself out of here right now, but I'm *not* a better man. In fact, I'm a weak man where this woman is concerned.

So instead of being noble, I close my eyes and fall asleep feeling the most content I have in a long time.

CHAPTER NINE

Mia

I wake to the sound of breathing, and I freeze.

I dreamt that Luke had come in here last night, and there's some vague memory about a rock-hard set of abs that I can't quite put my finger on.

I feel the rise and fall of a chest under my face and it hits me like a big yellow school bus that it wasn't a dream at all.

Luke is really in here – in my bed – and I'm cuddled into him like he's a cosy pillow.

I twist, just a little bit so I can look up at him.

He makes a sleepy groaning noise and wraps his arm tight around me.

My heart is beating so fast; this is so wrong, but it feels so right.

I shouldn't like the idea of him being here, in the bed I once shared with Troy, but I do.

I like it a lot.

I manage to shimmy his heavy arm down to my waist so I can look up at his handsome face.

I've always thought that Luke was a good-looking guy. When he turned up at our high school at the start of our final year, he could have had any girl he wanted, and he's only gotten better with age.

I can't see his eyes right now, but I can picture the shade of blue as if I was looking right into them.

His brown hair is dishevelled and in need of a cut, and his normally well-trimmed, sexy stubble is much the same. I kind of like him like this though, he looks rough and rugged and it suits him well.

I know I should probably get out of his arms and even further out of my bed, but truthfully, I don't want to. I want to stay right where I am.

I lift the blanket and peek at his bare torso.

I bite back a moan of approval.

The abs were *not* a dream. He's got a full set of the damn things.

I drop the cover back down before I start drooling all over him.

This isn't the first time I've seen him with a bare chest, but it's been a long time. He seems to stay covered up around me these days.

I realise now that it's probably because he's a gentleman, this current situation aside of course, and because he wanted me.

He wanted *me*.

He still does if the hand that's now under my top and rubbing at the skin on my back is anything to go by.

I timidly look back up to his face, which is now smiling at me.

"Good morning," he says, his voice thick and husky.

It sounds so sexy I find myself wishing I could hear it every morning.

"You're in my bed," I state.

MR. MARCH 63

He chuckles, and I feel it through my whole body. "I am. I'm sorry... I did ask, but I'm not sure you were actually awake," he replies sheepishly.

"I don't mind." I can feel myself blush at my confession.

"Good."

His eyes are blazing as they look into mine and I can feel tingles racing up and down my spine.

"My back couldn't handle another second on that couch," he murmurs as his hand reaches up to sweep my hair over my shoulder.

His fingers linger on my collarbone, tracing the shape.

I know he's about to kiss me, I can feel it in the air between us.

This is dangerous territory, but I don't want to run away, I want to go in all guns blazing.

"You are so beautiful, Mia," he whispers.

"You are too," I reply stupidly.

I see him grin at my comment.

I'm so nervous, I can't even think straight.

He's so close to me, our lips are only a fraction of an inch apart.

"Mia, Joe is awake and he's—"

The loud voice comes from the door and my stomach sinks.

"What the fuck is going on in here?" Everly screeches from inside my doorway.

"Jesus, Everly, haven't you ever heard of knocking?" Luke shouts at her.

She doesn't even hear him; her evil glare is locked on me like a lion about to attack its prey.

"Oh my god, you're sleeping with him, aren't you?"

"Everly," Luke warns her as I scramble to get away from him.

If I'm not touching him, maybe she'll stop yelling at me.

"Mia, it's okay." He reaches for my hand and I let him take it. I sit there, staring at him with wide, scared eyes.

"It most certainly is *not* okay," Everly sneers.

She takes a step towards the bed and Luke drags me behind his big body.

I know the old bitch in front of me isn't going to physically hurt me, but her words are like poison and I know she's only just getting started. I can still hear her from behind him, but Luke wants to do what he can to protect me.

I already know it won't be enough. Everly is a volcano that's about to blow and Luke and I, we're the small town at the bottom of the mountain.

"Troy is barely gone, and you've already moved on to his so-called best friend!" she yells – loud enough for the whole neighbourhood to hear.

I can't speak. She's right.

"Calm down, Everly," Luke demands.

"Don't you tell me what to do." She spits the words at him. "I wish it were you that died that day instead of him."

I feel the tears welling in my eyes. I'd never wish another person dead – not even the horrible woman in front of me.

"And you." She points a finger at me as I peek over Luke's shoulder. "You're nothing but a dirty little slut."

I'm shaking so hard and I can't make it stop.

I feel Luke tense in front of me. He's about to snap.

"You're a slag, a whore. Troy would be turning in his grave," she carries on, obviously unaware of the storm brewing inside of him.

"Mia," he says calmly – too calmly. "Go downstairs and find Joe, okay?"

He gets to his feet next to the bed and tugs on my hands to get me to climb off too.

I try to pull away from him, I just want to pull the covers over my head and hide, but I know he won't let me.

He reaches out a long arm and snags my robe off the chair by the bed and drapes it over my shoulders.

I push my arms in like a small child being dressed as he leads me past a still-screaming Everly and out the door.

"Find Joe, Mia, put his headphones on with Peppa Pig or something, okay?"

I nod at him, I can feel the tears streaming down my face.

He gives me a gentle nudge in the direction of the staircase and I take off running; I can't listen to that any longer.

I fly down the stairs, grabbing the iPad and headphones off the cabinet as I go past.

I can hear Joe in the kitchen; he's sitting at the table with a stunned-looking Robert.

"Mia, what is it?" he asks.

I shake my head at him and swipe at the tears running down my face with the back of my hand.

"Good morning, baby," I say to Joe. "I thought you might like some Peppa Pig while you eat."

"Peppa!" he cheers, seemingly oblivious to the screaming I can still hear from upstairs.

I tap at the screen and slip the headphones over his ears.

I sag into a chair in relief as his total attention is taken by the screen.

Robert gets to his feet.

"Robert, *don't*," I beg.

"What on earth is all the yelling about?"

I shake my head, fresh tears trailing down my cheeks.

"I'm sorry, Mia, but I'm going up there."

He walks out of the room in a hurry and I get back up to my feet.

I give Joe a kiss on the head and follow after him in defeat.

CHAPTER TEN

Luke

I take a deep breath in through my nose and blow it out through my mouth.

I count to thirty, giving Mia plenty of time to get Joe sorted out, before storming back into the bedroom.

I'm honestly surprised Everly didn't follow us out here, but when I lay eyes on her, it seems as though she hasn't even realised we've left.

She's screeching a string of curse words, none of which I'm about to sit back and listen to.

I've never, ever wanted to hit a woman before, and I know I won't do it now either, but this one *really* needs a slap.

"Shut the hell up!" I roar at her.

She stops dead in her tracks and spins around to face me.

I guess she heard that.

She opens her mouth to speak, but I cut her off. She's said enough already.

"Get out." I point at the door. "Pack all your shit and get the fuck out of this house."

"So you can live happily ever after with that *skank*? I don't think so," she spits back at me.

"I'm not fucking asking," I growl in a menacing tone I didn't even know I possessed. "You are going to pack up and get the hell out, and you won't be coming back here – not ever again."

"This is my son's house," she cries. "You can't throw *me* out."

"Not anymore it's not," I hiss. "Troy is gone, Everly. He's *gone*. And I know that you lost a son, but are you really so blind that you can't see what *she* lost? What we all lost?"

She glares at me, her face bright red from all her yelling. "It doesn't look like she had too much trouble replacing him."

I chuckle darkly. "It's been over two years. What do you want from her? For her to be miserable forever like you? For her to push away anyone that cares about her like you have? Is that what you want?"

He mouth opens and closes like a fish as she tries to decide how to respond.

Robert chooses that moment to enter the room, and I mutter a curse under my breath.

"What on earth is happening in here?" He looks between his wife and me for answers.

"The two of them," Everly sneers. "I caught them in bed together."

I could explain that I was only in here to avoid the couch, or tell them that Mia and I haven't slept together, but frankly, it's none of their god damn business. They can think what they like; it's no concern of mine.

The only thing I care about is protecting Mia and Joe.

I cross my arms across my chest and wait for him to throw in his two cents worth.

He doesn't – he just stands there staring like the pansy he is.

"I want you gone within the hour," I tell them both.

"You can't kick us out of here. Who do you think you are?" Everly cries.

"I *can*, and I *will*. I'm doing this for Mia and Joe. I'm responsible for them now and I'm telling you that it's time to go."

"Oh, you're *responsible* for them now, are you?"

I nod at her, one hard tip of my head.

"Is that what you call sleeping with your *best friend's* wife?"

I know she's trying to crack me with that, and on the inside, I feel it, but I'm not about to let her see. Instead, I smirk at her, which only angers her further.

"You two deserve each other. You're both trash. She was never good enough for him anyway."

"Mia didn't kill him, Everly, so stop making her feel like it's all her fault."

Robert tries to take Everly's arm, but she shakes him off. "Everly, let's just go," he suggests.

"You really think that's what Troy would have wanted?" She turns her rage onto her husband, and I almost feel sorry for him... *almost*.

I laugh darkly. "*What Troy would have wanted*? Are you kidding me? You think for a second that Troy would have let you talk to Mia like this? That he wouldn't have done *exactly* what I'm going to do, and thrown you out?"

She tries to cut me off but I'm not having it.

"Troy would have told you to take a flying leap, Everly. He was a good man and he loved Mia more than anything else in the world. He wouldn't stand to see her disrespected and neither will I. He loved her, and I've grown to love her the same way. Now get the hell out before I decide to call the police."

"You wouldn't." She gasps.

"Oh, believe me, I *would*."

Robert tugs on her arm and this time she lets herself be led.

I follow them with my eyes until they're out the door, and that's when I see her.

Mia is sitting on the floor, just inside the door.

"How much of that did you hear?"

"Pretty much all of it," she whispers.

"I'm sorry if I overstepped the mark. I probably shouldn't have spoken on your behalf."

She's hurting, I can see that in her eyes, but she still manages a beautiful little smile, one just for me. "*No* – you were perfect... I couldn't have said it better myself... thank you, Luke, you've always got my back."

I nod, but deep down I don't deserve thanking. I should have never let it get to this point. I should have intervened earlier. Everly has been looking for a reason to blow for a long time now, and I just handed her one on a platter.

"Get dressed, okay? I'll go down and sit with Joe."

She nods and gets to her feet.

I watch her walk slowly towards me before pushing up to her tip toes and kissing me on the cheek.

I've got one hell of an urge to grab her and kiss her the way I wanted to this morning before we got interrupted, but I know this isn't the time or the place.

This was a complicated situation before, but a whole new spanner has just been thrown in the works.

I already know this is going to do no favours for the two of us. Mia is a highly emotional creature, and this will hit her hard.

She wanders over to her drawers and starts pulling out clothes.

"Mia?" I say.

She turns back to look at me.

"You're not all of those things she called you. You're just Mia. And you're doing the best you can – which is amazing, Mia, *you* are amazing."

She looks like she might cry, and I'm about to apologise when she smiles and whispers, "Thank you."

***

I'm holding Joe near the door when Everly and Robert finally come downstairs, carrying their own bags this time.

"Say bye to Pop and Nan," I tell him.

He leans his little head into my neck and offers them a small wave by way of goodbye.

Mia is right next to me, and I'm holding her hand tightly in mine – I'm worried she'll run away if I don't.

She's shaking like a leaf now that Everly is back in sight, and I realise that letting Mia get away from her is exactly what I should be doing. I don't want to let them see that they've rattled her.

"You want to take Joe out back? I'll be there in a minute," I ask her.

She nods gratefully and takes him from my arms, carrying him outside without so much as a backwards glance.

I'm so damn proud of her for being the bigger person here.

She's too good to stoop to their level.

I open the front door and wave them through with my hand.

I wait until they're out on the front porch until I speak again.

"This is how this is going to work from now on. If you want to come to town, you check with Mia first, and you book a hotel. You will see Joe *if* and *when* it suits Mia, and if you come into her home, you will show her the respect she deserves. You understand?" I don't give them time to answer. "Failure to follow these rules will result in you not seeing your grandson for a very long time. Are we clear?"

I wait this time, my arms crossed across my chest and my brow raised.

Everly huffs out a breath and hisses, "Yes."

Robert nods sadly.

"Good," I reply before I slam the door shut in their faces.

I've got nothing more to say to either of them.

I catch sight of a framed picture of Troy on the wall as I turn around. "I'm sorry, man," I mutter. "I know they're your folks... but it had to be done."

I know kissing his wife is something that *didn't* have to be done, but I push it out of my mind. I'm tired for feeling guilty over something that I shouldn't.

It's like I told his parents – he's not coming back.

For whatever reason, he was taken from us and it's final. It's permanent. That's all there is to that story.

I'm here, and so is Mia, and I can't feel in the wrong for that any longer.

I don't want to feel bad for living and loving anymore.

I won't – and neither will she if I have anything to do with it.

I stride out back to find Mia and Joe.

CHAPTER ELEVEN

Mia

Luke is pushing Joe in his swing, and while he's doting on him entirely, his eyes keep seeking me out, searching for me, and watching me with an intensity I can feel all the way down to my toes.

"More!" Joe yells over and over, laughing as Luke swings him higher and higher.

I'm trying to busy myself in the garden, but I can't focus. Luke is too distracting.

I know he wants to talk about what happened.

I also know I'm using Joe as a barrier. I'm scared. I don't know what to do or what to say.

There was so much truth in what Everly said, and Luke and I, we're not even a thing... not yet anyway.

I know I *should* end it now, before it goes even more wrong, but just the thought of the small part of him I've been given this past week being taken from me, threatens to break me all over again.

I've already lost so much, I'm not sure I can handle anything more being ripped away from me.

I hate the universe for this – for taking my husband away and then dangling his best friend in front of me like some type of carrot with a six pack.

"Mia?" His voice comes from right behind me and I jump.

"You scared me," I murmur as I turn to face him.

I glance around and find Joe playing in the small sandpit that Luke built him last summer.

"Can we talk? I've let you avoid me for over an hour now."

I smile sheepishly. "Am I that easy to read?"

"You're like a book I've read a thousand times," he replies hoarsely, and I don't know why, but it makes me shiver.

"Come sit." He sits himself down on the swing seat in the sun, his long legs sprawled out in front of him, and pats the tiny space left next to him.

I sigh and tug off the gloves I've been using to garden.

I know I can't avoid him and this conversation forever.

I squeeze in next to him and he rests his arm around my shoulders, his thumb trailing lazily up and down my bare arm.

"I'm really sorry she talked to you like that, Luke," I say before he has a chance to speak.

"Don't be." He winks at me. "It's like water off a duck's back."

"Not for me," I admit. "I just wish she'd leave us alone, you know? It's like her sole purpose in life now is to hurt me."

"She won't hurt you again, sweetheart, I promise you that. I took care of it. You won't have to deal with anything like that from them ever again."

"I doubt she'll just give up... she gets too much pleasure from making me miserable."

"She can try," he says, "But she'll have to get through me first."

I breathe a sigh of relief that regardless of what happens, Luke is on my team.

This is yet another thing he has taken care of for me – the list is so impossibly long now that I've stopped attempting to count all the things on it.

"She's wrong, you know?" he says after a beat.

He uses his foot to push us back and forth gently on the swing seat.

"About what?"

"About *all* of it," he says simply. "This is *your* life, Mia, and you can live it anyway you see fit. Troy would have wanted you to live... don't let some stupid old woman stand in your way of having anything you want."

"And what exactly is it that I want?" I whisper. The minute the words leave my lips, I'm already afraid of the answer.

"*Me*," he says in a voice that is so pure and true, I've got no reason to doubt it.

"I wish it were that simple..." I sigh, Everly's awful yelling still ringing in my ears.

"People fall in love, Mia. I don't think anyone expects you to be on your own for the rest of your life."

I *haven't* been on my own though, that's the thing – I'm not sure I can even picture my life without Luke anymore. He's been here for everything that matters since Troy passed away. But that doesn't make me feel any better about the idea of changing the rules of our relationship.

"I know they don't expect me to be alone forever, but I also don't think that anyone expects me to shack up with you either, Luke."

"You know whose opinion I care about?" he says, utter conviction in his voice.

I bite down on my lip and wait for him to tell me.

"*Yours*, Mia... only yours and the few people that are welcome inside this house. That's it – no one else matters to me, they can think whatever they like as far as I'm concerned."

He's right. I know deep down he is, but I'm so torn.

"It's so hard, Luke. I feel unbelievably guilty."

"I do too. *Every single day*... but nothing worth having comes easy. And *you* are worth having. I know that for certain. The rest will figure itself out."

"Am I though? What if Emily hates me? What about Caleb?" I can feel my heart rate rising rapidly just thinking about what they'll say.

"You don't need to concern yourself with my sister, and Caleb won't hate you, Mia. He loves you and Joe."

"What if he hates *you* then?" I ask as I look up at him, knowing already that that scenario would be far worse. I couldn't live with myself if Luke lost or gave up friends or family for *me*. He's already given up more than enough.

He looks back down at me and reaches for my face, cupping my cheek in his big hand.

"It'd be worth it if I had *you*." He says the words in a voice so tender it fuses little pieces of my broken heart back together again.

"You are the best thing that has ever been mine, Mia. I know we're not together like that, but you and Joe... you're *mine*. I hate that the reason is because he had to go, but that's life, isn't it? It's hard. It's tough sometimes, but right here with you... it's worth struggling through it all."

My heart warms, because I *do* feel like I'm his. *We* are his and he's ours. It's the three of us against the world.

"You're so good to Joe and me. You do so much for us that's not expected," I whisper.

"I told you at Troy's funeral – I made him a promise."

"Is that the reason you're here now?"

I'm asking the question even though I already know the answer. He's not here out of obligation in the slightest – maybe he was in the beginning, but not anymore.

He shakes his head. "I'm here because I fell in love with you, Mia. I love you and Joe. I'm here because it's up to me now to show you that you're wanted and cared for."

I swallow deeply, trying to push down the lump in my throat, his words are too much. *He's* too much.

He makes me stronger and weaker all in the same moment.

He builds me up so I feel like I can take on the world, and then leaves me vulnerable in the very next breath.

"*You* are wanted, Mia. I want you like *nothing* else – I'll never let you forget it." It's a promise coming from his lips, I feel it.

"*Luke...*" I whisper.

He takes my hand in his and intertwines his fingers with mine.

"I know I'm not him, and I'm never going to be quite good enough for you, but dammit, I want you anyway. I want you to be mine in every sense of the word, even though I don't deserve you."

He's laying it all out on the table, being completely honest with me – not matter how ridiculous his truths might be.

Just the thought of Luke not being good enough for me is ludicrous.

If anything, he's *too* good. He's certainly too good for me... Luke is too good for *anyone*.

There's no one in the world good enough to deserve a man like Luke.

"You're more than enough for me," I tell him, and he smiles. He looks so handsome it literally takes my breath away.

"Tell me, Mia. Tell me what you're caught up on and I'll do my best to fix it."

I love him for saying that, but the reality is, there's some things even he can't fix.

"Troy," I answer with a quiver in my voice.

It's time to share my truths with him now. It's the least I owe him after everything he's done for me.

"It feels like I'm replacing all the memories I have of Troy with thoughts of you, Luke. My head is so full of you that I'm scared I won't have any space left in there for him." I can feel my bottom lip trembling, and I know it's not fair – what I'm saying to him – it can't be easy for him to hear, but that's the reality of my life, none of it is easy anymore.

"That's not what I want to happen," he tells me softly. "I don't want to replace Troy, and I *never* could. No one can take those memories from you, Mia, not even me."

"I just feel so *confused*. It's only ever been Troy since I was seventeen years old, and now there's you... and I don't know what to do with that."

Somewhere during this conversation I've broken eye contact and ducked my head in an attempt to hide from him. He's still rocking us slowly, and his hand is resting on my cheek.

He presses gently, tipping my face up so I'm forced to look at him.

"*I'm* here, Mia, *me*. I can't compete with a ghost, okay? But I can share with one... I want you to know that. I don't want to forget Troy any more than you do. He's a part of me too. I don't want that to change."

He leans down slowly and presses his lips to mine. It's not a hot and heavy kiss, but one that is filled with love and longing.

It's a promise-filled kiss.

"I'm going to go out for a few hours," he whispers against my mouth.

My heart sinks.

"Please don't go," I beg.

I can't bear the thought of him leaving me right now – I need him like I need to breathe.

"I have to," he says. It looks like it pains him to say it, but I know he's right. "You need some time and space to think – this has all come at you so heavy and so fast... I couldn't live with myself if I rushed you into anything."

He's leaving, and I know I shouldn't stop him – because the reality is, I could if I wanted to.

He'd do *anything* for me. Even stay when we both know he needs to go.

"I've made you so reliant on me, Mia, and I need you to decide that you want me here... whether that be as a couple or just as your friend. I'll be whatever you need, sweetheart, you just have to decide."

He places one more kiss to my lips and slides his big body out from next to me.

"Will you come back?" I ask, the desperation in my voice seeping out for us both to hear.

"Of course I will."

"Tonight?"

He nods and smiles at me as though he appreciates my eagerness to have him back, and the knot in my gut eases a fraction. "I won't leave you, Mia. I swear."

He goes over to Joe and ruffles his hair as he says goodbye.

As I watch him walk away, I feel a pang of something I can't place in my gut.

I know he'll be back – he said he would be, and he never lies to me, but this isn't fear that he's leaving, this is something else.

I can't figure out how it's happened so quickly, but it's almost as though these feelings have been lurking right there – hidden just below the surface and he's given me the chance to let them break free.

This is falling in love, my brain tells me.

Forget *falling* in love, I'm already there I realise as he disappears from sight.

CHAPTER TWELVE

Luke

"Hey, man, thanks for coming." I clap Dan on the shoulder as I come up behind him.

He was a friend of both Troy and mine in high school. He was Troy's friend first, but we got on well instantly and have stayed in touch over the years – even more so since Troy's been gone.

He's the only person I could think of that might possibly understand the predicament I've found myself in. He's also one of those few people I mentioned to Mia – the ones whose opinions I do actually care about.

"Anytime," he replies as he looks me up and down. "Is everything all good?"

I sit down on the stool next to him and wave the bartender over with my hand. "Why wouldn't it be?"

"It's not every day you call me over to the pub in the middle of the afternoon."

The bartender takes our order and disappears again.

I fiddle with the cardboard drink coaster on the counter in front of me as I debate how best to tackle this.

Having all those kids must have done wonders for Dan's patience, because he just sits there waiting for me to come out with it.

Our beers get dropped in front of us and I still haven't found the courage to speak about what I came here for.

He picks up his beer and takes a sip of it. "I'm not complaining, Kingy," he drawls, referencing the nickname for me that he's used since school, "it's still more relaxing here than at home, but you're starting to make me nervous."

"It's about Mia." I huff out a breath.

"Is everything okay?"

Everything is too good. That's the problem. *She's* too good.

"She's great, man. You should see her with Joe... she loves that kid; she's such a good mum." I know I've got a huge smile on my face as I talk about her, but I don't care – I'm here to talk to Dan about her after all so I may as well get on with it.

"Have you ever noticed how beautiful she is?" I ask him.

He chuckles. "Shit yeah I have. But you tell my wife I said that, and I'll knock you out."

I smirk at him.

"She's an incredible woman... she's sweet and kind, funny and warm. She's gorgeous and fun..."

"You sound like you're in love with her." He chuckles.

I meet his gaze with a sheepish look.

His eyes widen as he realises that he's not at all wrong and he nearly chokes on the mouthful of beer he just took.

"No shit?" he splutters. "You've got a thing for Mia?"

'A thing' is one hell of an understatement, but I nod anyway and let my head fall into my hands. "I don't know when it happened... just one day she wasn't my best bud's wife anymore. She was *my* best friend, and she was gorgeous and I just... felt it."

"Well fuck," he deadpans. "We should have ordered whiskey."

He gets it. I don't have to explain to him the implications of this. He already knows.

I know I've tried to make it clear to Mia that it doesn't have to be complicated, but inside my head, it still is.

I can push it aside when she's right there, but it's when I'm not with her that the real guilt and concern creeps in.

I tear at the paper on the bottle. Someone told me once that doing that is a sign that you're sexually frustrated, and right now I'd have to say they might have been right.

I haven't been with a woman for close to a year, but even if I'd been with one yesterday, if she wasn't Mia, I'd still be frustrated as hell.

There's only one remedy for me now – mind and body.

I think I'm craving the balm for my mind even more than I am my body.

"Does she know?"

I nod. "She had someone try to break in the other night and called me over in the middle of the night... I got caught up in the moment and hung it all out to dry."

"Did you sleep together?"

"Only in the literal sense." The corner of my mouth twitches into a small smile at the thought of crawling into bed with a half-asleep Mia. "I've kissed her, Dan. Nothing more. We've talked, but as I'm sure you're aware, this isn't your typical situation."

He doesn't reply. He's just sitting there with a thoughtful expression on his face.

"What are you thinking?" I question him.

"I'm just trying to think what I'd want for Leah and the girls if I died."

I wince. "I bet it's not for your best mate to shack up with them, is it?"

He takes a pull of his beer. "You know, I don't know. I'm not sure which idea makes me feel more uncomfortable, the thought of you with her, or the idea of a stranger playing daddy to my kids."

"The devil you know, or the devil you don't," I muse. "I've tried to put myself in his shoes, ya know? But I can't. I don't have a family."

We're doing that man thing right now, where you sit side by side and both stare forward, not looking at one another. I'm not great with sharing emotions in general – I'm fine with Mia – but as far as my male mates are concerned, it's a hell of a lot easier with no direct eye contact.

"But you *do*," he says after a moment of silence. "You have Mia and Joe. They're your family."

I feel like they're mine, I do. But they're Troy's first and foremost, and they always will be.

"You're the father figure in Joe's life, Luke. You're the one who helped Mia through the night feeds and the vomiting bugs..." He shrugs. "You're the one who Mia calls in the middle of the night."

I did do those things. I am that person for Mia, but it's not that simple.

"It feels like I'm stealing his family – like I'm benefitting from his death, as fucked up as that sounds."

He nudges my elbow and looks right at me. "I think he'd want you to be there for Joe. You were his best friend for a reason."

"So you think I shouldn't feel guilty?"

"I think you'll feel guilty no matter what I say. You've just got to decide if she's worth living with that guilt."

"She's worth it. *Undoubtedly*. They both are," I reply quickly. "I just don't want her to lose anyone else because of this. She's already lost Troy. She needs the ones she's got left."

"You seem pretty confident that she wants you the same way you want her?"

"I'm not confident at all... but sometimes I see the way she looks at me, you know? And I know we could make something of it. Something good."

"I can see you two together. You're strong where she's weak and I think she'd be good for you too – give you that sense of purpose you've been lacking."

She gives my whole existence a purpose.

"So the thought of it doesn't make you want to smack me out for shitting all over Troy's memory?"

He chuckles. "You're cutting his lunch, not shitting on his memory, man, and I just want you happy. Mia too. You both deserve a break, and if that's with each other then maybe that's the way it was meant to be. It'll take some time to get my head around it... but if that's what you both want, then I'll support you. *Always*. You know that. I'm certainly not going to be throwing any punches over it."

I can picture my whole life with Mia. I'm not stupid enough to believe that everyone will have as much of an open mind as Dan does, but it's maybe like that saying goes, 'those who matter won't mind, and those who mind don't matter', and it's like he said – if she's worth it, then I'll live with it.

"I appreciate that," I tell him gruffly, trying to disguise the emotion in my voice.

I sit the now-empty beer bottle down and shrug. "She might decide she just wants to be friends and this whole thing will be a moot point."

"I don't think so." He waves his hand to the bartender to bring us a couple more beers. "Mia adores you, bro, I've never looked at it as anything more than gratitude and friendship, but I think she'll get there, if she's not already. It's not a big leap to make from what the two of you have already."

I know what he's saying. That must be what happened to me. I slipped into love with her so naturally, I didn't even notice until it was done.

Two more beers appear in front of us.

"Game of pool?" Dan asks, and I grin.

I can't take much more of this deep and meaningful, I just need to hang out with a mate for a bit before going back to Mia.

"You're on."

***

I've been sitting on my third beer for an hour, and I've never been more ready to go home from a pub than I am now.

Dan is kicking my ass in our fourth game of pool, but at this point I think he's just killing time, making sure that his kids will all be ready for bed by the time he gets home so he doesn't have to do it himself.

"Just sink the eight already, we both know this game is over."

"Maybe you should spend less time playing house, and more time sharpening your pool skills," he taunts as he lines up the shot.

He hits the white ball with perfect precision and knocks the eight ball clean into the pocket, finishing the game.

"Hallelujah," I drawl.

I take his cue from him and slide them both back into the rack on the other side of the table.

"Your phone's ringing," Dan calls out to me.

I jog over but I've missed the call.

My screen shows a missed call from Mia.

I pick it up and I'm about to call her back when it beeps with a voicemail notification.

I dial through and block my other ear to try and hear what she's saying. The pub has started to fill up and it's fairly noisy in here.

"Luke, it's me... I'm sorry, I wanted to give you some space, but Joe is awake, and I can't settle him. He only wants you. I'm so sorry, but if you get this, please come home when you can."

I hang up the phone and grab my jacket from the back of the chair. "Mia called," I tell Dan. "Joe is upset and he's asking for me. I gotta go."

He shoots me a knowing smile. "Daddy duty calls."

"Something like that," I mutter.

I throw a wave back over my shoulder as I jog out the door.

All I can think about now is getting back to Joe and his mumma.

"Please come home when you can." Her voice replays over and over in my head as I drive down the darkened streets.

She asked me to come *home* and nothing has ever sounded so right.

I know I told her that I'd be whatever she wanted, but I don't want to just be friends. I don't want things to go back to how they were.

I want all of her. *Forever.*

CHAPTER THIRTEEN

Mia

He didn't knock. That's the first thought to cross my mind as he comes barrelling through the door, all six foot two of him.

I've been telling him forever that he doesn't need to knock, but this is the first time he's walked into my home like it's his own.

"We're in here," I call as he heads for the stairs.

I've got a whimpering Joe in my arms and no matter what I've tried, I just can't settle him.

Luke's eyes find mine before quickly moving onto the little boy in my lap.

He's in front of us in a second and stroking Joe's hair.

"Hey, buddy," he says softly. "What's the matter?"

"Wuke?" Joe asks, peeking out from under my arm.

"I'm here, bud."

"Wuke," he repeats as he holds his arms out for him.

My heart melts as Luke reaches for him and hugs him in his strong embrace. Joe will always be safe when he's protected by those big, broad shoulders.

"Do you feel sick?" Luke asks him.

Joe shakes his head.

"Did you have a bad dream?"

He shakes his head again.

"What's got you so upset then, bud?"

He's walking around the room, just holding him. He's so patient and caring – Joe is so lucky to have him in his life. I am too.

"I mwissed you," Joe says.

I can feel tears welling in my eyes as I watch the love between the two most important men in my life.

"I missed you too, bud," Luke tells him. "I don't want you to be sad though, okay? You don't need to cry, I'll always come back to see you."

Joe's not sobbing anymore – he's perfectly calm now; Luke's presence has given him the security he needs to relax.

I don't know how I can possibly repay him for that. He gives *me* that same security. He's the glue holding mine and Joe's lives together.

He's our rock – our safe place.

"*Mia*," Luke whispers and my head flicks up to look at him.

"Not you too," he whispers with a smile as he notices the tears that are now rolling down my cheeks.

I shrug helplessly.

"He's gone back to sleep," Luke whispers again.

He turns so I can see my son's sleeping face resting on his shoulder. He looks so precious and peaceful.

"Let's take him back up," I reply quietly.

We walk silently up the stairs to Joe's room and Luke lays him down in his bed and tucks him in under the covers.

"I'll never leave you, Joe," he whispers before kissing him on the head.

If I wasn't already falling in love with Luke, I would be after seeing that. It's the sweetest, most genuine gesture I've ever seen.

He creeps out of the room and grabs my hand as he reaches me by the door, tugging me along next to him and into the next room – my bedroom.

"I thought you'd want to stay close for Joe," he explains with a shrug.

He knows me so well.

He pushes the door so it's almost shut and I wander over to my still-unmade bed.

I can picture the two of us lying in here together. It's hard to think that it was only just this morning. It feels like a lifetime ago. So much has happened in the past twelve hours.

"Are you okay?" he asks as he sits down on the foot of the bed next to me. "I know you hate seeing him upset."

"I'm fine now." I smile up at him. "Thank you."

He takes my hand in his and brings it up to his mouth to kiss my knuckles. "You don't have to thank me."

I do have to thank him. I have so much to thank him for.

"He loves you so much, Luke. He trusts you with his life."

"I know," he replies simply. "I don't take that for granted."

"I trust you with my life too," I whisper.

He smiles at me like he's just won the lottery. "I don't take that for granted either."

"I feel like all you do is give, Luke, and all we do is take."

"You *give*, Mia," he answers gruffly. "Trust me, I get so much more from you and Joe than what I'm giving."

I huff out a disbelieving breath.

"Just because you don't mow my lawns, doesn't mean you don't give. You give me Joe… you give me *you*."

He's looking at me with a gaze so intense I can hardly stand it. He's too much again, but the last thing I want him to do is stop.

"I'm sorry." He shakes his head, seemingly disappointed with himself. "I told myself I wasn't going to pressure you any further one way or the other, but here I am, looking at you like you're the answer to all my problems."

"You're not pressuring me... you're just being yourself. Please don't stop," I almost beg.

The last thing I want is for him to stop being the person that I've grown to love.

He's something special, Luke Kingsford; he's smart, confident, travelled, and wise beyond his years.

He's looked death square in the eye so many times, it's like he's learned some secret about the world that I'm not privy to.

"I didn't come back here to talk about us, okay? I want you to know that. You need to think long and hard about this before you make any decisions."

I nod. I know I do.

I need to sleep on it.

That's what Troy always said. You have to give something at least twelve hours to stew. You don't make rash decisions; you have to give it time.

It's ironic really, that I'm taking my late husband's advice about the possibility of shacking up with his best friend.

"I'll go change the sheets on the spare bed, okay? I can't sleep another night on that couch. You should get some rest, you look exhausted."

I giggle and nod as he gives my hand one more kiss before getting to his feet and walking toward the door.

"Luke?" I call after him.

He stops and turns back to face me.

"Thank you – for Joe."

He smiles, his eyes lighting up. "Literally anytime, Mia. I love that kid."

He slips out the door and then he's gone. Leaving me with nothing but my thoughts.

***

"Luke?" I whisper into the dark room. "Are you awake?"

"I'm awake," he replies.

"Can I come in?"

"It's your house." He chuckles.

"You make a good point." I smile to myself as I creep into the room.

I can't see where I'm going at all.

He presses something on his phone and the soft glow shows me where I'm going.

"Can't sleep?" he asks as I approach.

I slept like a baby for the past six hours, but I woke wide awake and couldn't get back to sleep. I couldn't stop thinking about *him*.

"Something like that," I murmur as I reach the side of the bed. "Scoot over."

He chuckles again as he shuffles his big – half-naked – body over to make room for me.

"It's freezing, I'm coming in."

The light from his phone goes out as I pull the covers over myself and we're left alone together in the dark.

I feel him roll onto his side, presumably so he's facing me, so I do the same.

"Hey," he whispers.

"Hey," I reply.

I feel like a nervous teenager on her first date, lying here with him.

"You're not still thinking about Everly and Robert, are you?" he asks.

I've thought a lot about the both of them, but they're not what's keeping me up.

"No... I was thinking about *you*."

"You were?"

I don't have to be able to see to know that he's smiling, I can hear it in his voice.

"Mmm hmm," I reply. "I was thinking about what would happen if I run scared... if I were to keep you in the friend zone."

"And what would happen?"

"I was thinking that if I pushed you away you'd meet someone else eventually... and then I'd have to pretend I was happy for the two of you. I'd have to have you over for dinner and invite you both to Joe's birthday parties."

"You wouldn't be happy for me?" he questions.

I shake my head, even though he can't see me in the darkness. "I know I should say yes, but I wouldn't be. I'd be jealous."

"Why would you be jealous, Mia?" he pries softly.

He's having to drag the truth out of me piece by piece.

"Because I don't want you to be with someone else. I want you to be with *me*," I whisper.

He sucks in a deep breath and it's like he's just taking it all in – absorbing everything about this moment.

"I didn't even realise, Luke... how can you feel this way about someone and not even know it?"

"You were broken, sweetheart, your heart and your head have been through the wringer these past two years."

"I didn't even know I was looking for you," I confess.

"That's because you didn't have to look. I was already right here. You didn't have to look, I was waiting... for *you*."

I can feel my heart pounding against my ribcage.

This feeling of excitement feels foreign to me. I feel human again in a world where I've become accustomed to being numb.

"I was just lying in my bed... thinking about soul mates..."

"Okay... and what did you come up with?"

"I think it's bullshit."

He chuckles quietly. "Why's that?"

"People talk about the *one* perfect person for all of us... about our *one* true match being out there... but if that's the case then how come I got two?"

"You know what I think? You can have as many soul mates as you leave yourself open to... just because something ends, it doesn't mean it wasn't meant to be. Maybe it just wasn't meant to be forever."

I always thought that Troy and I were meant to be together forever, but maybe the universe had a plan all along. Maybe we were only destined for a small part of forever.

"I catch myself sometimes, Luke – I realise I'm not thinking about him... for the longest time, I couldn't think of anything else, but now it's like I have to make a conscious effort to remember him... to remember all of the things that he did. I don't know what's happened..."

"I think that's called moving on, Mia."

"I'm not sure how I feel about that," I confess with a whisper.

On the one hand, I'm happy to have the pain and the grief constantly on my mind, but on the other, I'm terrified that I'm forgetting the man who gave me everything.

"You're allowed to move on with your life, sweetheart, moving on doesn't mean you have to forget."

"I think I'm finally starting to understand that part of it... that maybe I might be able to make room in my heart for both of you."

"You *have* been doing a lot of thinking," he muses and I can hear he's smiling again.

It feels good to make him smile.

"I have. I thought that to give you my heart, I'd have to let go of him, but I think I was wrong. I think I can still give you my whole heart and still keep him in there too."

"Do you have any idea how happy I am to hear you say that?"

His hand finds my hip under the blanket and slides over it until his hand is resting against my lower back.

I giggle. "I think I might."

I half expect him to tell me that he loves me or kiss me to the point where I want to take off my clothes, but he doesn't.

Instead, he leans in and kisses me on the forehead. "Stop thinking for a few hours, sweetheart, I'm not going anywhere."

I might not be sure about a whole lot in my life anymore, but I *am* sure that he'll be here when I wake up, so I allow my brain to finally switch off.

I allow myself to feel content in his arms, with the wedding ring Troy slid on my finger all those years ago, on a chain around my neck.

CHAPTER FOURTEEN

Luke

It's only early. The sun is just beginning to rise in the sky.

I know I should get up and go for a run before I have to go to work, but I can't bring myself to move an inch.

I'm watching her sleep and committing every detail of her face to my memory.

I've looked at her hundreds and hundreds of times, but never quite like this.

I've never seen the freckles on her nose so close up, and I've never noticed the small, silver scar just below her hairline on her forehead.

I've never noticed the closed-up second holes in each of her ear lobes, or the way her bottom lip is just slightly fuller than the top one.

I've never looked at her when she's been in love with me.

She may not have said the exact words yet, but I feel them.

She loves me, and I love her, and after everything we've already overcome together, I'm pretty confident that love can get us through the rest – whatever that might be.

She opens her eyes sleepily and then shuts them tight again when she sees that I'm awake and watching her.

"I forgot you were one of those annoying morning people," she grumbles.

I prefer early mornings and early nights, while Mia prefers late mornings but also early nights. I've never known someone who values sleep as highly as Mia does.

"I'll let you sleep in." I chuckle as I roll over to get up.

"No." She reaches for me. "Don't go."

I lay back down, and she snuggles into my side.

"Please tell me last night wasn't a dream," she tells me with a yawn.

"What happened last night?" I feign confusion with a frown.

She looks up at me with worried eyes and I crack, smiling wide.

"That's not even funny, Luke," she grumbles, but I can see a smile playing on the corners of her lips.

"Ohh, you mean the part where you came in here and told me you were crazy in love with me?"

"I didn't say that." She giggles and smacks me lightly on the chest.

I move in a flash so she's on her back beneath me and I'm hovering over her.

I sweep some of her golden hair out of the way so I can look into her pretty green eyes without interruption.

"Well I'm crazy in love with you, Mia Vander."

She blushes and bites down on her bottom lip.

"I love you *recklessly*, Mia. I'll love you no matter the consequences."

"*Luke*." She breathes my name and it gives me goose bumps up and down my arms.

"Are you in with me? I know we've both got broken parts, and I can't promise that I can mend either of us, but I'll try. I'll spend every day trying, and I'll start right here and now by giving you all of me... Every last bit of me is *yours* if you want it."

She doesn't answer, just stares at me with so many emotions swimming in her eyes.

"What do you reckon?" I press.

My heart is beating so fast I'm on the verge of breaking into a sweat. Waiting for an answer from her is more terrifying than going into battle. It's more frightening than the possibility of losing my life, because *she* is my life now. Her and Joe are the most valuable thing I could possibly lose.

"I say *yes*. I have a feeling I'd say yes to *anything* with you," she replies in a sweet, gentle voice.

I know she's not just saying yes to a shot at a relationship, she's saying yes to a whole life together. This is permanent. She knows that as well as I do.

I also know that her telling me yes, is only the first of our hurdles to jump, but at least from this point onwards, we'll be coming at them as a team.

Because she said yes.

I can't believe how lucky I am.

I've never wanted anything as much as I want her, and it's not even just about sex.

I want to eat breakfast with her and fall asleep in her bed. I want to share day-to-day life with her – that's all I really want.

"I don't know what I did to deserve you," I murmur as I lean down and brush my lips against hers.

She giggles softly. "You did *everything*. You've put in two years of your life already, Luke... that's a lot of ground work. You did everything for me when I couldn't do it alone."

"I'm never going to let you be alone again."

"You promise?" she whispers.

"I promise."

***

"Hey, sweetheart, it's me, have you heard from Caleb today?"

I lean my hip against the fence I'm building for Mrs. Buttermore and wipe the sweat off my brow. It's a total scorcher out here today.

"I haven't. Is something wrong?" Mia's concerned voice asks down the phone.

"He didn't turn up for work this morning. I thought maybe he was just running late, but I can't get him on the phone and it's after two... I thought he would have shown up by now."

"That's not like him..."

I can hear the worry in her voice for her brother-in-law.

"I'm sure he's fine, Mia... something must have come up. Just let me know if you hear from him, okay?"

"I will."

"I've got to go home and get a few things, so I'll be back around four, alright?"

"I'll see you when you get home," she replies and this time I can hear the smile in her voice.

I love the way she calls it 'home' when she talks to me. I hope that one day she and I will share a home.

"Bye, Mia."

"See ya, Luke."

I hang up the phone and look up and down the street again, hoping that Caleb's truck will appear.

I've got so much on my mind right now, I can hardly focus on what I'm meant to be doing.

Even though I told Mia not to worry about Caleb, I *am* worried. He's never been late for work, let alone not shown up at all in the year and a half that he's worked for me.

He *always* answers when I call.

Something is definitely up, and I don't like it.

The other issue my mind keeps lingering on is the current living arrangement Mia and I have found ourselves in.

I've been staying at her place for coming up a week now, but I can't stay in her spare room forever – we both know it has to come to an end soon.

The problem is, I don't *want* it to come to an end. I want to be near her and Joe every day – not over at my house without them.

I don't want to come in too hot and heavy with her, but we need to have some discussions, and sooner rather than later as far as I'm concerned.

I roll out my shoulder and groan. One of my old Army injuries is playing up again, and with Caleb not here to palm off the heavy digging to, I know I'm only going to make it worse.

My body has been put through the wringer. I'm not even thirty and I've got more aches and pains than a man twice my age.

I'm physically fit and I know I'm in good shape, but it's not without effort and discipline; both of which I learned plenty of during my time served, and it's certainly not without discomfort these days.

The most traumatic of the injuries I received out there aren't ones you can see anyway – they're the ones inside my head and my heart.

I can sometimes still hear the sound of guns firing when I close my eyes at night, and I still wake up in a panic, on high alert as though I'm back in the danger zone.

I can still picture my best mate's face as he took his last breath.

The pain in my shoulder is nothing at all compared with those mental traumas.

I hit the number for Caleb and listen as it rings out over and over, the call going unanswered just like all the rest.

I huff out a breath and put my phone down on top of the fence.

I've got one more hole's worth of digging in me and then I'm going looking for him I decide as I drive my shovel into the dirt.

***

I grab my water bottle and down the entire contents in one chug.

I've just dug the last hole for the fence and if I never have to push a shovel into the earth again, it'll still be too soon.

My whole body is screaming in protest at the exertion, and I still haven't seen any sign of Caleb.

I *need* to find him.

There's an awful feeling in the pit of my stomach that is telling me something isn't right – that something bad is brewing.

It's the same feeling I got the day Troy died, and if nothing else, that experience taught me that I need to trust my instincts.

I grab my gear and start hauling it into the back of the truck. I don't know where to even start looking, but at least it'll feel a lot less like doing nothing than this does.

I climb into the driver's seat and start the engine.

I consider going around to his place, but if he's avoiding me – which I have a strong suspicion he is, then his house is the last place he'll be holed up.

I sit at a stop sign with my indicator flashing left, even though I'm not sure which way I want to go at all.

Think. I tell myself.

I refuse to think about the fact that something could have happened to Caleb – surely fate wouldn't be cruel enough to take both brothers.

"Where would he go?" I think aloud.

Caleb always asked Troy for advice when he was in trouble or needed help. If Troy were alive today, he would probably be talking to him about whatever is on his mind.

Troy.

That's when it hits me.

He will have gone to see his brother.

I turn the wheel hard to the right, in the direction of the cemetery and flick my indicator over.

I'm pulling out onto the road when I hear my phone beep with a new text message.

It could be Caleb.

It could be Mia.

It could be important, I reason as I grab my phone off the seat next to me and do something that I never do. I check my phone while I'm driving.

It's a message from Mia. I glance back at the road before pulling my eyes back to the screen in front of me.

From: Mia

Caleb is here. We're going for a walk.

Joe is with Maria, if you get home before me, pick him up, okay? He knows, Luke... about me and you.

Talk to you when you get home xx

My heart pounds in my chest as I drop the phone back on the seat.

"Shit," I mutter under my breath.

Well that explains why he didn't turn up for work today. I was right. Caleb *is* avoiding me, and something is wrong. Very wrong.

Mia needs me. She needs me right *now*.

I know Caleb would never set out to intentionally hurt Mia, but emotionally, she's fragile, and she's been through a lot these past few days without taking on any more from him.

I'm hit with a pang of guilt to the gut.

This is all my doing.

I've turned her life as she knows it on its head. I've stormed into her delicately put together world and made her question everything she thought she knew.

I pull the steering wheel around for a u-turn and plant my foot on the gas.

I don't even see the van coming in the opposite direction, not until I slam head-on into it.

CHAPTER FIFTEEN

Mia

I hear a car door shut from what sounds like my driveway and I glance at the watch on my wrist.

It's only 3.30pm, so either Luke is early, or I have an unexpected visitor.

I wander over to the front window and peek out from behind the net curtain. It's not Luke at all. It's *Caleb*.

My heart rate speeds up as I watch him look up at the house. His features look so much like Troy it gives me this awful sense of déjà vu all over again.

I love Caleb like a brother, but for no reason other than the way he looks, it was hard to be around him for those first few months after my husband died.

I found myself staring at him constantly and wanting to touch him. He reminded me so much of my husband for the longest time, I just had to stay away from him.

He steps towards the house and I get a feeling of unease in my stomach.

I can tell something is wrong, and in that moment, I just know. He *knows* about Luke and me.

That's why he didn't turn up for work. That's why he's *here* now. To confront me about it.

There's a knock at the door and I feel myself break out into a cold sweat.

This is exactly what I was afraid of. He's going to be so angry with me – and with Luke. He's going to be so disappointed in the both of us.

My head swings back and forth between the door and the front room where I can see Joe playing with his cars.

I don't want Joe to witness this; he's too young to understand why his favourite uncle will be mad at his mumma. He's too little to see us argue and fight.

I have to be strong, if not for myself, then for my son.

I take a big, deep breath and put on my big-girl pants. Luke isn't here to save me this time – I'm going to have to face this one on my own.

I can do this. I can keep this situation civil and under control.

I don't have to explain myself to him anyway. I don't have to explain this to anyone.

I love Luke and he loves me, and if Caleb or anyone else doesn't respect that, then they know where the door is. I repeat it like a mantra in my head, over and over, until I build up the courage to answer his knocking.

I swing the door open and my entire resolve crumbles.

Caleb has been crying. His eyes are bloodshot and he looks... *upset*... more so than angry, and I'm not prepared for that at all.

"Hey, Mia," he says, and his voice sounds as rough as gravel.

"Are you okay?" I reach out for his shoulder, but pull my hand back short; he looks like Troy again, and all of a sudden I feel light-headed.

"I'm fine," he tells me, but it's like I'm watching it through a haze.

MR. MARCH 109

I blink, once, twice, three times, trying to make my brain understand that the green eyes in front of me belong to Caleb, not to Troy, but I'm past the point of reason.

In my mind, *Troy* is in front of me and he's hurting. He's hurting because I betrayed him.

Luke and I... we made him cry.

"*Troy*... I'm sorry," I whisper.

I feel myself sway before everything goes black.

***

"C'mon, Mia, Jesus Christ, wake up already. I'm freaking out here."

My lids flutter open and closed again.

"Oh, thank god, I thought I was going to have to call an ambulance," Caleb tells me with a slight edge of hysteria to his tone.

Caleb says those words, *not* Troy.

I open my eyes again and look at the man crouched down next to me. Yes, his eyes are the same green, but they're rimmed with a hint of gold that Troy's weren't; *yes,* they have the same jet-black hair, but Caleb's is longer and shaggy, where Troy's was always cut short and tidy, and Caleb has a thick beard on his face where Troy was always clean-shaven.

This isn't Troy, it's *Caleb*, and I feel like a fool.

"What happened?"

"You passed out." He's looking at me with concern in his eyes. "I caught you when you fell – you didn't hit your head or anything, but you were out to it for a long time... Maybe you should see a doctor?"

"I'm okay," I tell him.

At least I think I'm okay – if not a whole lot embarrassed.

"Joe." I push myself up in a rush, suddenly panicked about just how long I've been out for, and my head spins.

"Relax, Mia, he's fine. I told him you were taking a nap and I took him over to Maria's next door. He's eating cookies and colouring in."

My body sags back down to the couch in relief.

"I'm sorry, Caleb, I… I… I'm not sure what happened."

He looks at me with sad eyes. "You thought I was Troy."

"I don't know what went through my head." I sigh.

He sits down on the edge of the coffee table and looks right at me.

"You panicked."

"You'd been crying… I thought you knew… it was like it was him… oh god I'm so sorry," I ramble.

"I *do* know, Mia…" he replies quietly. "I know about you and Luke."

I know it's not the question I should be asking, or what I should be saying, but it's what finds its way out of my mouth first as I squeeze my eyes shut tight. "How did you know?"

"My parents." He says the words as though they're causing him physical pain.

"Oh shit," I mutter.

I don't know if I'm more terrified about the version of events that his awful mother is likely to have given him, or angry that he had to speak to her at all because of me.

"They called you?"

"*She* not only called me but turned up at my place this morning."

"They're still in town?" I wince.

"It would seem so."

I groan and cover my face with my hands. "What did she tell you?"

He doesn't answer me after a long, long pause, so I peek out at him from between my fingers.

"Are you still dizzy?" he finally asks.

I shake my head.

He holds out his hand to pull me up and looks at me with sad eyes.

"Can we go for a walk?"

***

We've walked about four blocks in total silence.

It's as though neither of us knows what to say or how to start this conversation that we desperately need to have.

I glance at the 'for sale' sign on a beautiful old house that I've always admired as we walk by. I could picture myself living in a place like that, but I've always been too nervous to really consider selling the house that Troy and I bought together.

I smile to myself. I don't feel so scared about the idea now, and I know that's got a lot to do with Luke.

The only thing I'm scared about when he's around are how quickly my feelings are growing and how little control I have over them.

But he's not around right now, and I'd only be lying to myself if I said I didn't fear this conversation with the man next to me.

"*So...*" Caleb finally says, breaking the silence between us, and I sigh.

"So..." I repeat back to him.

"You and Luke?"

"I guess so." I shrug. "It's a really new thing."

"Mum said she caught you two in bed together."

"Caleb, I—"

"I'm sorry, I shouldn't have said that... you don't need to explain, Mia. You're both adults and quite frankly, Mum is a bitch."

I let out a nervous giggle. "She's *something* alright."

He shoots me a sympathetic look, and I'm grateful for the fact that no matter how disappointed or angry he is at me, he still isn't going to try to justify the actions of his mum.

"I'm sorry that you had to find out like this, we wanted to tell you ourselves, but we haven't had a chance, you have to believe me when I tell you that this is a new thing... It just sort of *happened*."

I look up at him and he nods but doesn't say anything in response.

"I'm sorry that you got dragged into your mum's drama."

He huffs out a breath. "You know, it's the first time I've seen her in *ages*, and she didn't once ask how I was, or if I was seeing anyone, or ask me what I was doing for work. It was all about Troy... and how the two of you had *betrayed* him and *tarnished* his legacy."

His words drive a knife into my gut. I might be able to forget about what Everly said to me, but I don't know how to deal with the obvious pain she's caused Caleb.

He's been like a little brother to me for a long time.

He's three years younger than me, and I've watched him grow up since he was a fourteen-year-old, with pimples and greasy hair.

Troy and I were teenage sweethearts and I spent a lot of time at his family home – and with Caleb – so I care a lot about the young man in front of me, and I hate seeing him so obviously hurt.

"I'm sorry," I choke out. "I didn't mean for any of this to happen."

He laughs humourlessly. "Don't be. My mum's a bitch, Mia."

"You know that's not what I'm apologising for," I whisper.

He nods again and falls silent. We walk another whole block without saying a word. I can tell he's thinking, I just have to hope that he'll talk when he's ready.

"You know, I was mad as hell when I found out."

I can feel myself breaking out in a sweat again.

"I was angry at you, and Luke. I couldn't understand how you could do this to Troy."

"Caleb, we—"

He holds up his hand to stop me from saying any more. "Please, Mia, just let me get this out."

I snap my mouth shut and wait.

"I was *so* mad. I nearly went to work and punched Luke... He kept calling and it just made me more and more angry. I wanted to come over to your place and yell at you – or shake some sense into you... but I knew I couldn't do either of those things. So instead, I went out to the cemetery and just sat there and told him all of it. I know he can't hear me anymore, Mia, but I didn't know where else to go."

I know how he feels. I've spent countless hours at that very headstone, telling him everything there is to tell about Joe and I... telling him everything he's missed out on.

I can feel the tears welling in my eyes as Caleb speaks. I want to say something, *anything* to make him feel better, but I don't. He's asked for my silence and that's the least I can give him.

"I'm hurt, Mia, I don't know how else to explain it."

I *hate* that I've hurt him.

Anger from his mother was bad enough, but *hurt*, that's something different.

I love Luke, I really do, but I'm not sure I'm strong enough to deal with this.

I can feel my pulse quickening and my heart feels like it's trying to jump out of my chest.

I want to run, but my feet won't move.

"I'm sorry," I whisper, because I can't think of anything else.

"I don't know what I'm supposed to say." His voice sounds defeated. He sounds like he's running on empty.

I don't know what to say either. All of a sudden I feel like I'm running on empty too.

The vibration of my phone ringing in my hand startles me. I glance down at the screen, but it's not Luke's name flashing across it like I'm expecting it to be.

"I better get this," I tell Caleb as I hit 'answer' on the call from the private number.

"Hello?"

"Hello, I need to speak to Mia Vander please."

"Speaking," I answer as I glance up at Caleb.

He's standing still, and it's only then that I realise I've stopped walking. I can't explain the feeling of unease in my stomach, but it's there.

"This is Olivia, calling from City West Hospital emergency department – I'm one of the nurses here, I'm afraid I have some unwelcome news for you."

My whole body tingles with awareness as I process what she's saying.

"Oh my god, *Joe*." I clap my hand over my mouth as panic sets in.

My baby. Something is wrong with my baby.

"Mia?" Caleb questions as he reaches for my arm; his face looks how mine feels.

"No, ma'am," the woman on the phone tells me. "The patient's name is *Luke*. Luke Kingsford."

Relief floods my system momentarily, before panic sets in again.

Joe might be fine, but Luke *isn't*.

"*Luke*," I whisper as fear takes over. "Is he okay?"

"I'm going to need you to come down to the hospital, Mia. As soon as you can get here."

I feel faint again. I can feel the darkness seeping in around the edges the same way it did earlier.

The entire street feels like it's spinning. I don't know if I'm awake or asleep right now, but I still have it in me to curse myself for being so god damn weak and fragile.

"Luke is in hospital." I say aloud. "No, no, no, no..."

There's a feeling, like a weight pressing down on me, threatening to crush me.

"*Mia*," Caleb says, "Luke needs you, we have to go." The mention of Luke's name is enough to pull me out of my trance.

The man who has taken care of me through everything needs *me* to help him now.

I blink once, twice, three times before taking off at a run down the street.

CHAPTER SIXTEEN

Luke

A try to suck a deep breath into my lungs and groan as my ribs scream in protest.

I bring my hand up to my face and tug on the tubes that I can feel stuck in my nose. I don't like the feel of them. I want them out.

"Uh, uh, uh," a voice tells me as I feel a small, warm hand covering mine. "You still need those."

It's the voice I know like the back of my hand. The same one I'd recognise anywhere, even in my dreams.

"*Mia*?" I ask; my voice sounds scratchy and my throat feels dry.

"I'm here," she says, and I feel the warmth squeezing my hand again, only gently, like she's afraid she might break me.

"I'm right here," she says again, and this time it's almost a sob of relief.

I open my eyes and blink a few times, trying to make out my surroundings. It feels like I've been asleep for a long, long time, but I'm still struggling to keep my eyes open.

"Where am I?" I ask as they fall closed again.

"You're in the hospital, you were in an accident," she tells me, her voice so soft and gentle. "You got pretty banged up, but you're going to be okay."

As soon as she says it, I remember.

I remember the impact. The sound of metal slamming against metal.

I remember the van.

My eyes fly open and I try to push myself up to a sitting position. "The other driver, are they okay?"

Her hands are on my chest in a flash, preventing me from trying to climb out of bed.

She's not particularly strong but combined with the pain thrumming through me at the sudden movement, and the concern in her eyes, I don't try to push it any further.

"He's fine. Just a few cuts and bruises. You came out worse off."

I release a breath I didn't realise I'd been holding in.

If someone had died out there, I don't know what I would have done.

"It was my fault. I was distracted looking for Caleb and then I got your message and I was so worried. I didn't look hard enough."

I can hear the panic rising in my voice.

"I didn't even see the van until it was too late."

"Hey," she soothes. "It's okay. He was speeding, it's not all your fault. There was no way you could have seen him in time – distracted or not."

A nurse comes into the room and effectively ends our conversation. "Good morning, Mr. Kingsford, I'm glad to see you're awake."

It occurs to me then that I don't even know what day it is. I don't know how long I've been in this bed or even what's wrong with me.

"How are you feeling?" she asks as she picks up my chart from the end of the bed and starts scribbling down some notes.

"Sore," I say.

"I can give you some more pain relief?"

I shake my head. I've dealt with worse pain in my life, and any more relief will only make me sleepy. I need to find out what I'm dealing with before I go back to sleep.

"What's wrong with me?"

She looks up from her notes and then glances at Mia, who gives her a nod to go ahead and tell me.

"You've got a fracture to your arm and ribs, a badly sprained ankle and wrist, a couple of nasty gashes that have been stitched up, a concussion and a whole lot of bruises. But all in all, nothing too major; you were lucky, all things considered."

I nod my head as she lists off my injuries. She's right, it's not too bad. Nothing that a few weeks off my feet won't fix.

"You're going to need to take it easy for a little while, but there's no reason you shouldn't make a full recovery. We'll just need to keep an eye out for infection – some of those cuts were quite deep."

"I'll take care of him," Mia tells her. "I'll make sure he doesn't over do it."

"Okay good." The nurse smiles at her before turning to me. "She's the boss, you got it?"

I try to raise my hand to salute her, but it's obviously my sore one, because pain shoots up my arm and I wince.

"Alright, more pain relief for you," she announces.

I protest, but I'm outnumbered by the two of them, and before I know it, everything feels a little bit fuzzy and warm again.

I don't know what they're giving me, but it must be some good shit because I'm pain free in an instant.

The nurse has left and it's just Mia and I in the room again.

She leans over and gingerly lays her head on my shoulder, being careful not to hurt me at all.

"You put *me* down as your emergency contact." She's not asking a question, but merely stating a fact.

"Of course I did. You're the most important person in my life," I whisper as I close my eyes.

"You scared me," she says, and it's the first sign of real fear I've heard in her voice.

"I'm sorry."

"You can't leave me, Luke. I need you. You made me a promise. I don't care what anyone says or thinks… I love you."

"I'm keeping my promise, Mia. I'm not going anywhere. It'd take a lot more than a speeding van to keep me from you."

CHAPTER SEVENTEEN

Mia

I step outside the door and take a big, deep breath of fresh air.

I can't erase the vision in my mind of him lying there, unmoving and pale, surrounded my machines and medical professionals.

The fear I felt was so real and raw, it still causes me to break out into a cold sweat whenever I think about the possibility of losing him.

I hate hospitals something fierce, but I've been inside one for two days now, because no matter how much I dislike being here, I'd never leave Luke alone.

I spot a small garden with a bench and wander in the direction of it.

Luke is asleep, so I've probably got half an hour before I need to head back up.

I pull out my cell phone to call Emily and check how Joe is doing, but when I look at the screen, I see she's beaten me to it.

There's a bunch of photos of what he's been playing with and a rundown of everything he's eaten this morning already. She's even informed me of his poop schedule.

I have to laugh at that over share. When I told her I wanted to know everything, I didn't expect her to take it quite so literally.

Emily has been an absolute godsend.

She's insisted that I stay here with Luke while she takes care of my son. I would have understood if she wanted to be here at his bedside herself, but she's declared that I'm the one he needs right now.

I never considered that someone might actually be happy about Luke and mine's relationship, no questions asked, but *she* was. In fact, forget happy, Emily was ecstatic, and not in the least bit surprised.

That's what I love about Luke's sister – she's a total free spirit who doesn't want or need to think twice about something like this, or see it as any type of problem.

She's just happy that we're happy. End of story.

I sigh as I think about the fact that not everyone is so accepting.

I know I'm going to need thicker skin, because nothing and no one is going to stop me from being with Luke. Getting that call and seeing him lying in a hospital only cemented the fact that I *won't* be apart from him.

The sun warms my face as I sit out here and a small bird lands near my feet. I watch it as it hops around before flying away.

I look down from the sky where I watched the bird disappear and catch sight of Caleb. He's standing outside the hospital doors looking lost.

"Caleb!" I call to him.

He looks around for who called his name. His face morphs into a sheepish expression when he recognises it's me, like he's been caught doing something he shouldn't be.

He walks slowly over to me and I shuffle over so he can sit down next to me.

"Are you here to see Luke?"

"Is he okay?" he asks instead of answering my question.

"He'll be fine in no time."

He nods his head but doesn't say anything more.

We sit in silence, but unlike last time we spoke, I don't feel nervous about it.

"Mia," he finally says. "I'm sorry for how we left things."

"You don't have anything to be sorry for."

He turns so he's looking right at me, rather than looking everywhere *but* at me, like he has until this moment.

"I couldn't understand how the two people that were the closest to him could be together like that, and it took me a day or two, but I think I *finally* get it... it's *because* you were the two people that were closest to him."

His words bring a tear to my eye.

"I can't help but think that this is exactly what Troy would want. I know that sounds weird, but he's not here anymore and he would have wanted you to be happy. He loved you so much, Mia."

"I loved him too. I still do. That's why I've felt so guilty," I confess.

He reaches out and gives my hand a reassuring squeeze.

"He trusted Luke more than anyone in the world. Can you think of a single person he'd rather you and Joe were sharing your life with? Because I can't."

"No," I answer honestly, because there isn't another answer. It was Troy's final wish – that Luke would look after us. He gave him the burden of that responsibility because he knew Luke could shoulder it.

"I'm not going to lie to you, Mia, it hurt. It still hurts a bit, but I get it. You're entitled to get on with your life – I don't want to punish you for being alive; that's what my mother has done to all of us, and it's not right."

He's right. That's exactly what Everly has done to me, Luke, and to him too.

"I don't want to feel guilty anymore. I know Luke carries it with him every day and I'd give just about anything to take that away from him. Not just the guilt for having these feelings, but his guilt for not being able to save Troy too."

"You *can't* take that away from him, only he can let that go... he's a good man, Mia. Luke is one of the best guys I've ever met, and he'll look after you with everything he's got. I can see how much he loves you and Joe. He'll take care of you both better than anyone else ever could."

"Thank you." I sniff back the tears that have snuck in. I'm feeling totally overcome with emotion at his honesty.

I didn't expect him to take it this well or to be this kind.

This is the best outcome I could have hoped for from him. He's upset, but he doesn't hate me or Luke. He's hurt, but he's willing to be compassionate and he's trying to understand.

He shrugs. "Troy never held a grudge, and I'm trying to be more like him."

I know that Troy would be so proud of the man that Caleb is today.

"So you'll keep coming over and hanging out with me and Joe?" I ask as I wipe the tears away from the corners of my eyes.

"Just try and stop me." He grins.

That's all I want. I just want life to go on.

I just want to be happy.

"Thank you for always being here for me, even when I pushed you away."

"I get it – I look just like him… I know how hard that was for you." He looks at me with sympathy and understanding in his green eyes.

"You *knew* that was why I couldn't look at you?" I ask in surprise. I thought it was a secret I had kept well, but clearly, I was wrong.

He nods sadly and then gives me a smile. "Why do you think I grew a beard and caveman hair?"

I don't know why, but that makes me burst into laughter. Crazy, almost hysterical laughter just bubbles from me.

He made himself look like Tarzan, just to make life easier for *me*.

Caleb looks at me with a smile. "It's good to see you laughing, Mia. Even if that laugh is kind of scaring me."

A feeling of peace settles over me in that moment as I sit here laughing with my brother-in-law, and I find myself looking up to the sky.

I don't know what I believe anymore; whether there's something more out there after you're gone, or if you can look over the ones you love, but I don't think it matters what I believe anymore. I just have to do what's best for me and Joe and try and let the rest go.

Troy and I had the best life together and now it's time to see what Luke and I can share.

***

I step inside the small hospital room and have to do a double take of the scene that's greeted me.

I could be imagining it, given that I haven't had a lot of sleep these past few days, but when I hear Luke say my name, I know that it's really happening.

Robert is sitting next to Luke's bedside, looking cautiously across the room at me.

"*Robert*?" I blurt out in surprise.

"Hi, Mia."

I look to Luke for an explanation, but he just shrugs at me.

I haven't got the faintest clue what Robert's doing here, or more to the point, how he managed to convince Luke to let him stay, but I guess I'm about to find out.

"Are you here to see *me*?" I ask in confusion, as both men watch me enter the room.

Robert clears his throat. "I came to see how Luke was doing, and I wanted to talk to you too, yes." He shrugs. I can tell he's embarrassed and perhaps a little nervous too – I know I certainly am.

"Come here, Mia," Luke says, and I scurry across the room to his side.

He smiles up at me and holds out his hand for me to take. I grasp it in mine gratefully as I sit down as close to him as I can.

I feel ridiculous. He's lying hurt in a hospital bed, and I'm still looking at him to take care of me. Even though there's no sign of Everly here today, I still feel a little on edge.

I don't know if Robert is here to yell, or judge, or to apologise even – this thing could really go any which way and I try to mentally prepare myself for any of the possible outcomes.

I feel Luke's hand tighten around mine and it's only then that I realise my eyes are squeezed shut tight.

"You're okay, sweetheart." He murmurs his reassurance. "It's just him here."

I can do this. This will be my first attempt at having thicker skin. I open my eyes.

Robert is sitting opposite me, on the other side of Luke's bed, looking at me with sadness.

"I'm really sorry for what happened with Everly, Mia."

I shrug my shoulders. "You're not responsible for her actions," I tell him softly.

"*No*, I'm not," he agrees, "but I am responsible for mine, and I never should have let things get this bad – I should have said something to her a long time ago."

"You're right. You should have," Luke almost growls from next to me.

Robert's gaze flickers from mine to Luke's and back again.

"She's put Mia through *hell*. I get she's been hurting, but we all have, Rob, and what she's done isn't right." He coughs a bit and I reach for him in concern.

His ribs are fractured and he shouldn't be stressing like this.

"I'm okay," he says in reply to my unspoken concern.

Robert looks at him as though it hurts him to witness Luke's pain. "You're right. It's *not* okay, and I'm sorry for that, Mia – you too, Luke."

Luke squeezes my hand and gives him a nod.

"Thank you. I appreciate you coming here to tell us that," I say.

Robert gives me a small, sad smile. "She's not the same woman anymore. She changed when Troy died, and she's just become this awful version of herself that I don't know how to deal with."

"Why don't you leave her then?" Luke asks, his question mirroring my thoughts.

Everly is *horrible* and Robert doesn't deserve the wrath of her any more than I do. I can't fathom why he continues to put up with her moods and abuse.

He shakes his head. "I've thought about it, believe me... but I *can't* leave her. She's not the woman I've been married to for thirty years, but that woman is still in there somewhere – she has to be. I think I just need to hang in there and wait for her to come back to me."

I don't know whether to admire his commitment to his wife, or shake him for being so god damn stupid, but it's his life – it's his choice to make. I hope he'll afford me the same courtesy with my life and my decisions.

"But regardless of the status of our marriage, I still need to apologise for the hurt she caused – she had no right to judge you, *either* of you. I know you loved Troy, Mia. But the reality is that he's not coming back, and the last thing he would have wanted is for you to never move on with your life."

"I know." I smile sadly.

Robert clears his throat awkwardly again and gets to his feet. "Well, that was all I really came here to say. And I'm glad you're okay, Luke, I really am."

I nod at him as he walks towards the door.

I could just let him go without saying another word, but if I'm going to try and honour what Troy would have wanted then I have to speak up.

"Robert?" I call after him before he disappears around the corner.

He turns back.

"You're welcome to see Joe as often as you like, okay? Troy would want him to know you… just give me some notice before you come, and we'll sort something out."

He smiles for real this time. "I'd like that. And we'll be sure to book a hotel in the future."

"I think that would be best." I manage a smile.

He disappears out into the hallway and I sag against Luke in relief that it's over and it didn't result in any screaming or yelling.

"That was not what I expected," I murmur into his shirt.

"Are you okay?" He chuckles.

"I'm fine. I'm exhausted. I'm relieved. I'm in love." I list off all the things that I'm feeling.

"That was really big of you, Mia. Troy would be proud of you."

"Thank you," I murmur, "I just hope they give us at least a couple of months breathing room."

"Well, I get out of here tomorrow, so maybe things can go back to normal for a while before the mother-in-law from hell graces us with her presence again."

"I don't even know what normal is these days," I say with a smile.

There's a knock at the door and when I look up, it's Caleb standing there.

"Hey," Caleb says to Luke.

"Hey, man," Luke replies, a hint of caution in his voice.

These are the first words that have been exchanged between the two of them since things have changed.

I watch Caleb's expressions carefully. I know he's told me he wants us to be happy, but I don't know how he's going to handle things with Luke yet.

It's a complex, sensitive situation we've all found ourselves in, not helped in the least by the fact that Luke is broken and bruised.

The silence stretches for a few long moments before Caleb blows out a deep breath and finally speaks. "I'm so fucking glad you're okay."

I can almost see the weight being physically lifted from his shoulders.

I'm so happy he decided to come up here after all.

He crosses the room until he's standing in the spot his father just vacated.

I hear Luke say something to Caleb and a mumbled reply back that I don't catch before Luke pulls Caleb in for one of those semi awkward man hugs that involve a lot of patting each other on the back and not a lot of actual hugging, but it's still a sight for sore eyes.

I release a breath I hadn't realised I'd been holding. I'd have felt terrible if their bond was lost or damaged over something like this. Caleb doesn't have a lot left of his childhood relationships – he needs *both* Luke and I in his life.

"I better get going, Dad's waiting. I just couldn't leave until I saw for myself that you were alright."

"You came with your dad?" I ask in surprise. He didn't tell me that part when we talked outside.

He nods. "We're speaking again... spending some time together."

"I'm happy for you, Caleb," Luke says, and he sounds like a proud big brother.

Caleb shuffles towards the door, gives us both an awkward wave and disappears.

I smile up at Luke and his answering smile is blinding. Maybe things might be going to be okay after all.

CHAPTER EIGHTEEN

Luke

This whole 'live in your own house away from the woman you love' thing, isn't all it's cracked up to be.

I've endured less than *one week* of being back home and I'm sick to death of it already. It's not that I particularly enjoyed being stuck on Mia's couch half the day while she waited on me and played nurse, but being all healed up and home on my own isn't all that great either.

The only positive is that it's the weekend now, and it's time for me to surprise Mia.

I'm taking her on a date – technically our *first* date.

It feels weird to call it a first date when I already know everything about her, but that's exactly what it is.

Just because we're going about this in a way that isn't by the book, it doesn't mean I don't want to do things right by her.

I want to treat her, spoil her and woo her. I want to make her fall even deeper in love with me than she already is.

I knock on her front door and wait, even though I know it drives her crazy – if I'm honest, that's why I do it – I like seeing that adorable little crease that forms in between her eyes when she frowns at me.

She opens the door with that very frown in place, but before she can tell me off, I get in first.

"You ready, Mia?" I grin at her.

"Ready for what?"

"It's date day."

Her confused face morphs into a thrilled one. "We're going on a *date*?" she asks excitedly, her voice rising a few octaves.

God, I'll take her on a date every weekend if she's going to get this excited about it.

"We sure are... but not until later. You have plans for the afternoon first."

"I do?" Her eyes widen with surprise.

I nod. "I'm watching Joe, and you and Em are going to get pampered." I point out to my car where Emily is sitting, waiting for her. "So, go on – get out of here."

"But... *what*?" Mia asks. "I'm not ready."

"You don't need anything but you."

"But Joe?"

"I've got Joe covered, sweetheart. Just go and have some girl time. You deserve it."

I give her a little push out the door and in the direction of the car.

"I need my bag," she argues.

"No you don't. This is on me. All of it."

"Luke you can't—"

I grin at her as she tries to turn back and argue with me. "I already did," I interrupt her protests. "All I need you to do is make sure my sister doesn't ding up my car or get any speeding tickets. Alright?"

I steer her towards the vehicle by her shoulders.

I open the door and all but put her inside.

"Are you sure?" she asks as she does up her belt.

I chuckle. She's so sweet. I know she hates taking handouts from anyone, but I can see how excited she is about this afternoon. Mia never treats herself or takes time out for her, but all that is about to change. I'm here to take care of her now.

"Look after my girl, Em."

My sister salutes me and gives the engine an impatient rev.

"Jesus," I mutter under my breath. My sister isn't exactly known for being the most level-headed of drivers.

I give Mia a quick kiss on the lips before I shut the door and then they're gone.

I grab the bag I left on the step and head off to find my favourite little man.

***

"We're baaack," I hear with a giggle from the entry of Mia's house.

I smile – just hearing her is enough to make me happy. "Mumma's back," I tell Joe.

His little face breaks out into a grin and he gets to his feet and rushes from the room, following the sound of Mia's voice.

I glance around at the huge race car track we've set up on the living room floor and chuckle. I'm not sure which one of us was having more fun with this project.

Mia appears in the doorway with Joe on her hip, and I can physically feel my eyes bulging out of my head as I look her up and down.

She looks unbelievably *gorgeous*.

She's had her hair, makeup and nails done today, plus a massage and whatever else my sister managed to milk out of my credit card. There's a twinkle in Mia's eye that I haven't seen for a while.

She looks like she's finally living again. She looks *happy*.

"Jesus, Mia," I breathe. "You look beautiful."

She might be wearing makeup, but it's not heavy enough to hide the blush on her cheeks as I admire her.

"You spoilt me," she scolds in a voice that makes it obvious she's not actually mad in the slightest.

Emily appears in the doorway, looking as relaxed as I've ever seen her. "We got the works," she announces triumphantly.

"I'm sure you did," I muse.

Unlike Mia, Em is more than happy to spend my money.

I ignore my sister and approach Mia. "Seriously, sweetheart, you look incredible."

"Thank you." She bites down on her bottom lip nervously.

"Look how pretty your mumma is, Joe."

"Mumma pwetty," he parrots.

Mia's smile widens.

I cup her face gently in my hands and really look at her beautiful eyes. They look so much brighter and alive framed with thick, dark lashes.

"Did you have fun?" I ask her quietly, doing my best to have a private moment with her even though my sister is still lingering like a bad smell.

"It was the best, thank you, Luke, you always know what I need."

"Aww you two are so cute," Emily gushes.

She reaches for Joe and tugs him out of Mia's arms. "C'mon, Joe Joe, let's give these love birds some private time."

"Where da bwirds?" Joe looks around animatedly at the prospect of doing some bird spotting.

I chuckle at Em having to explain that there aren't actually any birds.

"We trashed the living room."

Mia doesn't even glance around to inspect the mess, instead she steps in closer to me, and fists my shirt in her hands. "Good," she whispers.

I'm still holding her face and I'm not sure I'll ever be able to let go.

I lean in slowly and brush my lips against hers. "I missed you."

"I missed you too." She giggles quietly. "It seems silly, but I spent half the time I was away thinking about what you and Joe were doing back here."

"Well if it makes you feel any better, he didn't ask about you once," I reply with a grin.

"Luke!" She lightly smacks my chest. "That's mean."

I shrug. "The kid loves me, what am I meant to do about it?"

She giggles. "I can't argue with that."

"Go get dressed," I whisper as I kiss her again, deeper this time.

"I haven't been on a date since high school," she replies quietly.

Since *Troy*, I think to myself. But I don't say it. I know Troy will always be a part of our lives, and I wouldn't have it any other way, but tonight, just for this *one* night – I want it to only be about Mia and I.

"Well, put on something nice, because I'm taking you out."

"Where are we going?" she asks, excitement dancing in her eyes.

I laugh. "You know I'm not going to tell you that."

She pouts.

I turn her around and point her in the direction of the staircase. "And pack a bag. If it's okay with you, I'm going to keep you until tomorrow."

She turns back around and gapes at me.

I know she's going to ask about Joe, so I get in before she can.

"Em and Caleb have agreed to stay over tonight and look after Joe together – he's in good hands."

I expect some kind of argument, but what I get is the opposite.

She claps her hands together excitedly and rushes off up the stairs.

It's only then that I realise this will be the first night that Mia has had away from Joe in the two years he's been here.

She's well overdue for a break. Even though he's the coolest kid in town, he's still a lot of work, and Mia is here doing it on her own most of the time.

But she won't be on her own much longer – not if I have my way.

CHAPTER NINETEEN

Mia

I smooth down my dress over my thighs as I glance nervously back at Luke.

He looks *so* handsome. He's had a shave, and what was fast becoming an unruly beard is now trimmed, sexy stubble.

His hair has been cut and styled.

I'm not the only one who got cleaned up for tonight.

He looks seriously gorgeous.

I almost feel guilty – not for betraying Troy this time – but because I've somehow managed the good fortune of having two handsome men love me, where others have none.

"Are you hungry?" He smiles at me as he notices my ogling.

I'm starved, both for food *and* for him. The thought makes me blush and he grins wider, almost as though he can read my thoughts.

"Sure am," I reply with a nervous giggle.

"You're nervous," he states.

I nod. "I'm freaking out."

He shakes his head in amusement. "You know me, Mia, I come over more than twice a week... well, when I'm not injured... I bring you flowers every Tuesday. We've basically been dating for a long time now." He chuckles. "There's nothing to be nervous about."

"But this is *different*." I wince. "This is a *real* date."

He takes one hand off the wheel and reaches over to squeeze my leg.

"I think it's cute."

"I think *you're* cute."

He chuckles and puts his hand back on the wheel. "You're damn right I am." He grins, looking thoroughly pleased with himself.

It makes my heart feel happy to see him like this. I know I've had struggles over the years, but Luke has too. He's worn a lot of the responsibility of the life Troy left behind, but with very little of the rewards that go with that life.

I don't think of myself as a prize of any sort, but it's clear that Luke does, and if being with me makes him feel like this – happy and content – then it's a win-win situation as far as I'm concerned.

He doesn't seem to see Joe and I as an obligation or a chore, he sees us as a trophy he can't wait to collect.

It shocks me, how much love I feel when I look at him, but there's no denying it now.

It'd be like trying to live without breathing.

Impossible.

I've never been blind to the connection between us, but I guess I wasn't looking at it from the right angle... or maybe I had my eyes shut.

I don't know what the reasoning was... but I see it now. And now that I've seen it, I can't look away.

"We're here," he announces, and I realise I've slipped into a Luke-filled day dream yet again. It's becoming a frequent occurrence for me.

I really am like a teenager all over again, all I need now is a notebook to doodle his name in with a bunch of love hearts scrawled around and the whole package will be complete.

He stops the car and gets out to open my door for me. He's only got a slight limp as he walks now, his bruises have faded and gone and his cuts are nothing more than shiny scars now.

I just about drool at the sight of him in his navy blue suit and crisp white shirt as he rounds the hood.

He looks *incredible*.

I might feel like I'm sixteen all over again, but this is certainly no teenager holding his hand out for mine.

Nope, Luke is *all* man.

He's looking at me with that expression I can't place as I step out of the car.

It's intense, too intense to look right at, and it's focused solely on me, like the rest of the world doesn't even exist anymore when he's looking at me the way he is now.

"Why are you looking at me like that?"

His mouth curves up into a smile, but his eyes don't soften – they're still smouldering.

I feel like a zebra, waiting for the lion to close in and devour me.

"I just can't get over how mouth-watering you look." He almost growls the words at me. "You've got no idea what you're doing to me, do you, Mia?"

To be fair, I could probably make a pretty educated guess, but I wouldn't feel comfortable making the assumption. It still shocks me to the core that *I'm* here... *he's* here... that we're here *together* because he was able to see the woman underneath the broken pile of rubble.

Not only did he *see* me, but he's spent so much time putting me back together piece by piece. What once seemed like a mountain of destruction is only a small pile now – and that's mostly in thanks to him.

"You are so god damn sexy in that dress."

I tug on the hem nervously. I haven't worn a dress this short since before I had Joe, and my body isn't exactly the same as it used to be.

"Leave it," he murmurs as he leads me towards the door. "You look incredible."

"Are you sure it's not too short?" I murmur nervously.

He pulls on the handle and gestures for me to go in ahead of him – always a gentleman.

"As far as I'm concerned, it's not short enough," he replies with a cheeky grin.

It's incredible how his smile can relax me.

I've barely stepped inside and he's right there next to me again, his big warm hand making my skin tingle even through the fabric on the back of my dress.

"Table for Luke Kingsford," he tells the woman behind the small counter with a charming smile.

"Mr. and Mrs. Kingsford," she says, "right this way."

I know I'm not Luke's wife, but I don't bother correcting her, and much to my surprise, neither does he.

***

"Do you ever miss it?" I ask as I sip my glass of wine. "Or think of going back?"

I know it's a bit of a loaded question, given that Luke's exit from the Army was made earlier than anticipated and far more dramatically than what it should have been.

He and Troy had both enlisted at the same time, at nineteen years old and worked their way through the ranks. Troy was a corporal and Luke was a specialist and medic.

They started together, progressed together and should have left together – I guess technically they did, but Luke came back on his own two feet, while Troy came back in a box.

He sits down the bottle of beer he's been drinking from and cocks a brow at me.

"The Army?" he asks.

I nod.

"God no." He shakes his head as though the very idea of going back makes him shudder. "I have no desire to be a soldier ever again, Mia."

"It can't have been all bad..."

"It wasn't," he replies quickly. "It's nothing against the Army at all, sweetheart, it's just... it's not for me anymore. I made some great buddies over the years and I learnt some irreplaceable skills... I got to help a lot of people and serve our country, but I'll never go back."

"Why?" I cock my head to the side and watch him with intrigue. I can see he's not particularly comfortable talking about this, but I want to know everything about him, the good, the bad and the ugly. I want to see it all.

"Other than losing Troy... I learnt it wasn't for me – that life. I like some space to breathe and there's always someone right next to you in the Army. I learnt a lot about myself in those years... I didn't want the military to *become* me. I wanted to explore the world and one day find someone to share my life with. I saw how hard it was for Troy and the other guys with wives and kids to leave on each deployment. I didn't want to be that kind of dad or husband."

"You had plans to pursue something in the field of medicine when you got out," I prompt.

I know he had plans. *Big* plans… to travel and study. Plans that didn't include babysitting his best friend's widow and child.

"Plans can change in the blink of an eye," he says with a shrug, as though giving up everything he ever wanted doesn't faze him in the slightest.

"I don't want to be the reason that you didn't do all the things you wanted to do, Luke."

Someone walks past the table and his eyes dart out to look at them before finding me again.

I'd forgotten where we were, that we weren't alone here.

I've learnt that Luke has the ability to do that to me. He makes everything else slip away until it's just him and I.

It's a dangerous concept that I feel myself craving.

He reaches across the table and takes my hand in his – his thumb gently stroking up and down my skin.

"But you *are* the reason." There's so much intensity swimming in his eyes that I can't even find it within me to argue with him about his response. "You're not holding me back from *anything*, Mia…" he says quietly. "But you have changed my mind about what it is I want. Believe me when I say I'm not missing out on anything… everything I want lives under your roof."

"What about seeing the world?" I whisper. I'm so overwhelmed by his confessions that my voice has decided to abandon me.

"It's not going anywhere." He shrugs. "Maybe one day we'll go and see it together."

"I'd like that."

He grins at me and it makes my heart falter. "Don't you worry about me, Mia, I'm perfectly content."

"What about your dreams of being a medic?"

Luke would have been smart and dedicated enough to be a doctor if he wanted to be, but he's told me on more than one occasion that that's not what his dream was.

He liked being the first point of contact in a crisis. He wanted to be able to do something for someone that needed it urgently.

He's always been a bearer of hope.

"I'm not saying *never*, but not right now. It's just not something I could do at this point in my life."

I nod and give his hand a gentle squeeze.

I don't push him any further on it. I know the reason behind that already. Watching your best friend die and not being able to do a thing to stop it is bound to change your perspective on everything.

He wouldn't be human if it hadn't made him revaluate his priorities. It certainly made me take another look at mine.

"Enough about me, what about you, Mia? You always wanted to be a vet nurse, when are you going to follow your own dreams?"

I knew it was only a matter of time before he turned this interrogation session around on me, and it would seem that time has come.

He's right – although I'm certain I haven't spoken to him about my career aspirations for years – I always wanted to be a vet nurse.

In fact, I even did two years of study before Troy and I moved out here and bought the house.

I put my study on hold to work so that we could afford the place, and the intention was always that I'd go back and finish my qualification once Troy retired from the Army.

Obviously that part never happened.

It's been over two years now, and I know I can't stay at home with Joe forever, but I wish I could. He's only got one parent, and I don't want him to feel like he's been pushed aside by me.

"I still need to finish my study... Maybe when Joe goes to school I'll find the time."

We've been living off the payout we got from the military when Troy died. His life insurance took care of the mortgage and our credit card debt, so Joe and I get by okay, but it's not a permanent solution by any means.

"You could study part time, from home." He picks up his beer and takes a long drink as I watch him carefully.

He's making the suggestion so casually, but something tells me he knows more about this than he's letting on.

I raise my brows at him and he grins sheepishly as he drops the bottle from his lips.

"I might have asked Em to look into it for you."

I shouldn't be surprised – his consideration knows no bounds – but somehow, I still am.

It never occurred to me that he would even think about my future in this way.

"I'm not saying you should jump into it, but you should think about it, Mia. Joe could go to a day care for a couple of afternoons a week and interact with some kids his own age, and I could help you out whenever you needed me to."

"You've thought a lot about this." I giggle nervously.

He holds up his hands and makes a small gap between his thumb and forefinger. "Just a little bit."

The idea may have only just been put into my head, but the more I think about it, the more I want to make it work.

I've not done a lot of anything for myself since Troy died – other than say yes to whatever this is with Luke – but this is something I should consider, not only for me, but for Joe too. For our future.

I'm suddenly overcome with the feeling of wanting to kiss Luke. I don't want to be sitting across from him in this fancy restaurant any longer – no matter how delicious the food was, I'm ready to go and be closer to him.

"You want to get out of here?" he asks, as though he can read my mind yet again.

"I sure do."

"Come take a walk with me, Mia," he says as he gets to his feet and offers me his hand. It's more than a walk he's offering, I can sense that, but that only makes it more appealing.

I reach out and take his hand in mine with absolutely no reservations whatsoever.

CHAPTER TWENTY

Luke

I smile at Mia's wide eyes in the dim light of the park.

We've been strolling hand in hand around this lake for what feels like forever, neither of us in a rush to be anywhere else.

This isn't like any date I've ever been on – this feels more like a married couple getting a rare night off from their kids than it does a first date.

I think I actually like the sound of that even more.

I thought I already knew everything about Mia, but I was wrong. Sure, I knew most of the important stuff, but we've been out here sharing every little, insignificant detail, and I've learnt so much already.

She wanted a huge family before, but now she's not so sure.

She's never swum in the ocean because she's terrified of sharks.

She snuck into a movie without paying when she was fifteen and she still feels guilty about it.

She'd really love to get a dog.

This is just a handful of the new information I've been privileged enough to receive, because that's what learning about her is, it's a privilege that not many people are privy to.

I sling my arm over her narrow shoulders and kiss the top of her head.

She's wearing a pair of heels tonight, which makes a rare change from her Converse, so I don't have as far to lean down to reach her.

She's incredibly petite and fragile looking, and I worry that even the weight of my arm might be too heavy for her small frame.

"Have you decided what you want to do about Joe? I don't want him getting upset or confused if he sees us kissing."

It's been playing on my mind a lot lately – how to approach him with this new relationship.

Mia laughs, surprising me. "Don't worry about Joe."

"I *always* worry about Joe." I chuckle.

She stops walking and turns to face me, her arms winding around my middle.

"He's *two*, Luke, and he adores you. It's not like you're some new guy on the scene that he doesn't know. You've been there with him since he was born – let's just let him watch things evolve naturally and if he's got questions when he's older then I guess I'll worry about that then."

"*We'll* worry about that then," I correct her. "I'm not going anywhere, Mia, you have to stop talking about us like we're temporary. I'll be there for these conversations. I'll be there for everything."

There's only the light of the moon and the dull glow of the park lights, but I can still tell she's blushing.

We haven't exactly discussed what we are, or put a name on it, but I can tell it's time. Mia obviously needs the reassurance.

"I *don't* think we're temporary." She shakes her head gently. "But I guess I'm not sure that I believe anything is permanent anymore either."

"*I am*," I murmur as I run my hand slowly up and down her arm. "*I'm* permanent. You couldn't get rid of me if you tried."

"I wouldn't dream of it." She sighs.

"You're mine now, Mia. I'm yours. We're together. So whatever that means to you – it's yours. You want to call me your boyfriend, partner, sex slave... *whatever*..." I grin. "I'm down for it. I don't care what you call me as long as it translates to being yours too."

"Good," she replies quietly as she reaches for my neck and wraps her hands around.

She's so unbelievably beautiful when she looks up at me with her big green eyes. I'm so far gone on this woman I can't find my way back – I don't want to either. I've never been so happy to be lost.

I lower my head and kiss her with everything I have – showing her how much she means to me with every brush of my lips and flick of my tongue.

She makes a sweet, breathy sound as I pull away.

I know she's no stranger to the fact that I love her, but it feels like I've never really had 'that moment'... that moment where I get to say those words to her and she really feels them.

Right now is that moment.

"Mia?"

I don't know why I prompt her, she's looking right at me.

"Mmm?" she murmurs.

"I love you."

She smiles shyly, and I can tell how much she likes the sound of those words.

"I love you too, Luke."

Now I'm the one smiling, and I'm not afraid to show it. I could listen to those words on repeat for days and still never grow tired of hearing them.

"Take me home," she whispers.

***

Mia's been to my place before, but she's looking at everything as though she's seeing it for the first time.

She's looked at every photograph and read the spine of every book.

She's nervous.

So am I.

We haven't discussed sex at all, but I think we both feel that it's brewing between us.

I can't take my eyes off her and that dress she's wearing isn't helping the situation in the slightest.

Neither of us has said a word for a full ten minutes. I'm standing here, watching every tiny move she makes like she's the most fascinating creature I've ever come across.

She looks back at me over her shoulder and smiles, and just like that, I can't stand the space between us a minute longer.

I cross the room and wrap my arms around her – her back is pressed against my front.

I kiss her shoulder, and she tilts her head to give me better access to her exposed skin.

I trail kisses up and down her neck, smiling as my stubble has her shuddering and giggling.

Her hand winds its way into my hair and her fingers pull gently at the strands.

Every sense I have is on high alert, and they're all tuned into her.

She's got me completely sucked in.

Her scent, the feel of her body, the sound of her moans, the taste of her and the sight of her bare skin are all I'm aware of.

"I've never seen your bedroom," she whispers suggestively.

She hasn't. It's a situation I need to remedy immediately.

I run my hand slowly down her shoulder to her wrist and take her hand in mine. I lead her from the living area and down the hall with only one destination in mind.

I push the door open to my bedroom and step back out of the way so she can enter.

I'm expecting her to take total stock of everything in here, like she did the living room, but she doesn't. She takes two steps inside and turns back around to face me. She's barely looked at the room – in fact she's not looking at anything other than me.

I step towards her and she slides her hands under my jacket, helping me to shrug it off.

I watch her fingers make short work of each of the buttons on my shirt until it's hanging open in the front. She tugs the hem loose from my pants and runs her hands over the groves of my chest and abdomen.

I finish the job for her and my shirt drops to the floor in the same way my jacket did.

I run my finger over her collarbone and over the thin strap of her dress, pulling it with me as I go.

I repeat the action on the other side and lean my head down to kiss her soft, creamy, skin.

Her grip tightens on my waist as I reach around her to lower the zip on the back of her dress.

"I hope you don't mind what you see," she whispers as I finish unzipping her.

She's looking into my eyes with so much worry and concern it hurts me.

"My body isn't what it used to be... Since having Joe..." Her voice trails off.

That's when it occurs to me that she's never shown herself to anyone as she is now. Not even Troy has seen her body since she grew a human inside of it, and maybe it makes me a bit of an asshole, but I'm glad we get this – this little piece of untouched is only *ours*.

"Your body is *beautiful*."

"You haven't seen my stretch marks..." she whispers.

She's wrong, I *have* seen the small, faded lines on her stomach. She can't reach the top cupboard in the kitchen without her shirt riding up, but I'm not about to admit that I've been perving on her when she's not looking.

"I don't care about your stretch marks, Mia. You grew a baby to get those marks – they only make you more beautiful in my eyes."

"But what if you don't find me attractive... in that way?"

"That's never going to happen."

"You don't—"

"Why don't I just show you," I interrupt her by sliding the straps of her dress even further down, tugging the fabric from her body as I go until she's standing before me in nothing but her underwear.

"I think you should know, I don't go past second base on the first date," she whispers with a coy smile as I undress her.

"Lucky this isn't really a first date then, huh?" I growl. "Because those eyes of yours are begging me to make a home run."

She grins at me and looks down at my body, so I do the same, laying eyes on her for the first time.

Nothing, and I mean *nothing*, could have prepared me for the sight in front of me, and it's got nothing at all to do with stretch marks, and everything to do with how sexy she is.

This is by no means the first time I've seen a woman in her underwear, but I haven't had much in the way of girlfriends over the years, and I've certainly never had feelings for any of them the way I do for Mia.

Even if she wasn't drop dead gorgeous, it wouldn't matter, because I'm in love with this woman, and I'd still want her more than anything else.

"Excuse my language," I growl at her, "but you are fucking *stunning*."

She giggles and blushes. "I think I can handle a curse word or two."

"And I can handle a stretch mark or two."

She rolls her eyes and grins. "*Alright*, touché, Mr. smooth. Enough of that talk."

"I think I'm about done talking altogether," I breathe as my lips brush against hers.

"I think that's a smart choice," she whispers, a slight tremble in her voice.

I take a deliberate step away from her and slowly unbutton my pants and lower the fly.

She watches with eyes full of heat and desire as I let them fall to the floor and step out of them.

All I'm wearing now is a black pair of boxer briefs... and my socks.

I chuckle as I look down and she follows my gaze before giggling too.

I toe off my socks and then we're just standing there, each of us taking our fill of the other.

I want to close the gap between us and rip the underwear from her body, but I won't.

Mia deserves to be adored and cherished, and I'm the man for the job.

I want to take my time with her so I don't forget a single detail. One thing I've learnt is that life is short, but there are some things that deserve a long, long moment of that life.

This is one of those things.

Mia is one of those things.

I'm here, ready and willing to give her as many of my moments as she wants to take.

I'm so caught up staring and thinking, that it's her who takes the first step.

She presses her warm, bare skin against mine and I hear a sigh of satisfaction. I'm not even sure if it came from me or her.

"Don't break me, Luke," she whispers as I reach behind her and undo the clasp of her bra.

"Never," I whisper back as her thumbs hook into my boxers and slide them down my thighs.

I sweep her hair from her shoulder, so it falls loosely down her back.

My fingers drag down her spine from her neck to the sway of her lower back and she arches into me.

I can feel the rapid thrum of her heartbeat against my chest and it makes me smile – mine is doing the exact same against hers.

My fingers toy with the band of her thin underwear before shoving them down over her ass and thighs.

She wiggles free of them and immediately I've got her in my arms without conscious thought. My wrist protests a little, but I ignore it. Mia's worth a little pain.

Her legs wrap tightly around me, and my hands grip her ass.

I already knew this was permanent between us, but as I lower her down onto my bed and sink deep inside her, it feels yet another step up from permanent… if that's even possible.

It feels *eternal*.

CHAPTER TWENTY-ONE

Mia

The grey knit jumper Luke gave me to put on falls down near my knees, like a big oversized dress.

It's heavy and a little scratchy against my skin, but it's warm and it smells like him, so I might never take it off.

He is downstairs getting food.

I might not have dated in a long time, but it seems that part hasn't changed. Sex still makes men hungry.

I grin to myself as I hear him clattering around in the kitchen.

That was some seriously *incredible* sex. The intensity inside that man is something I've never encountered before. He sees me – really sees me, and he doesn't shy away from showing himself to me either.

I loved Troy with everything I had, and our sex life was nothing to turn your nose up at, but I never connected with him on that level.

If Troy took me to the top floor of the building, then Luke just made love to me on the freaking roof.

I shake my head as my mind relives every touch of his fingers and brush of his lips.

I revel in the fact that surprisingly I don't feel an ounce of guilt. A touch of sadness perhaps, but no guilt.

What just happened felt so right it couldn't possibly be wrong.

Everything with Luke feels right, and I can't argue with that. I don't want to.

Luke appears in the doorway then, his hand gripping a chicken leg that he's gnawing on.

He holds it out to me, offering me a bite.

I shake my head and giggle. "That's okay. You have it."

He grins at me like that was the answer he was hoping to get.

I turn back around and continue my exploration of his bedroom.

You can tell a lot about a man by his bedroom and I want to know everything about Luke.

I wander over to the dresser in the corner of the room. I can see a few framed photographs, and I'm dying to know who is important enough to him to hold pride of place.

The first one I see is of Luke and Emily at her graduation. He's wearing his full military uniform and he looks so handsome and proud of his sister.

My eyes linger on it a moment before moving to the next.

My heart swells in my chest at the sight of the three-image frame. They're all of Luke and Joe.

There's one photo from when Joe was a little baby. I think I might have even been the one to take it. Luke is asleep in the recliner chair, with Joe sleeping on his chest.

The next is when Joe was about one and Luke took him to a car museum. Joe is grinning with excitement and pointing to one of the shiny vehicles.

The last was taken only a month or two ago. Joe is on Luke's shoulders, his arms out wide like an aeroplane. He's not gripping onto Luke's shoulders like you see most kids doing – it's like he has complete trust that Luke would never drop him.

I took that photo too, in my back yard, and I've seen the very same picture tucked in Luke's wallet.

Seeing the three images here together, it hits me again just how good Luke has been to Joe and me over the years.

He's *always* been there. Every single step of the way.

Joe might not have had his biological father there, but he's had one hell of a surrogate one.

I can feel tears welling in my eyes, ones of pure happiness, and I'm about to turn around and thank Luke for being exactly who he is, when the last photo on the dresser catches my eye.

It's me.

Not only me, but Luke and Troy too.

I reach slowly for the frame, as though it might disappear into thin air in front of me.

I've never seen this photo. I can't even place where it was taken.

I can feel Luke watching me from across the room as I stand there, holding the frame in my hands, staring at it.

"That was taken the weekend before Troy and I got deployed for the first time. You remember we went to that bar and got rolling drunk?"

I *do* remember now that he's reminded me. Flashes of it anyway... I was the most drunk of the three of us unfortunately.

I strain my memory to try and go back to this point in time, but I can't place the exact moment this picture was taken.

I'm in the middle of the three of us, Troy is on one side and Luke is on the other. My arms are slung over both of their shoulders and I'm lifted clean in the air – they're both so much taller than me, even as teenagers.

I'm looking at Troy like I worship the ground he walks on and he's smiling at the camera, but what really takes my breath away is the way that Luke's head is thrown back in laughter.

He's so carefree and happy.

There isn't the weight of the world on his shoulders in the way there has been since he returned from his last tour.

"Who took this?"

He chuckles from across the room and I hear him walk towards me.

He comes up behind me and wraps his hands around my middle.

"You remember that awful girl I dated after high school?"

"*Brittany*?" I ask, screwing my nose up. That girl really was awful.

He chuckles, and the vibration sends shivers down my spine.

"Yeah *her*. She turned up that night, do you remember?"

I give a noncommittal shrug. This is why I don't really drink – I couldn't handle my alcohol back then and I'm no better now.

He laughs again. "You spewed all through your neighbour's rose bush. God, that was one hell of a night." I can hear the smile in his voice and even though this is pure embarrassment for me, I still find myself smiling along with him.

He has that effect on me.

"Yeah, yeah, I seem to remember that part..." I raise a brow at him. "Let's get back to Brittany the bitch, shall we?"

He kisses the top of my head and chuckles. "She must have held onto it a long time, she sent it to me after Troy passed away. I had no idea it even existed."

"That was nice of her," I reply quietly as I stare at the picture again.

"I guess she's not so much of a bitch these days."

I giggle. "I *really* like this picture."

"It's the favourite of all my photos," he replies simply.

I can see why. It's such an accurate representation of the fun we used to have back then.

"It's the history of us," he says, his thoughts mirroring mine. "The *three* of us."

"Will you make me a copy?"

"I'll do you one better," he says as he places kisses to my neck. "One day soon, maybe I'll let you share that one."

It should surprise me, this obvious hint about us moving in together, but it doesn't. I know Luke like I know the back of my hand.

I want him around as much as I can have him.

I want to share my life with him even more than I have the past two years.

The only skeletons in his closet are the ones that we share, and that probably shouldn't be reassuring to me, but it *is*.

We'll fight our demons together.

CHAPTER TWENTY-TWO

Luke

I've always thought the idea of a person changing someone with love was a bit of a cop out, but I understand it now.

Mia has changed me in a lot of ways, but I feel it most in these past two days since we slept together.

We're joined now, I can sense it.

I know I've got a stupid grin plastered across my face, and a glint in my eyes, and I couldn't care less.

I'm more than happy for the whole world to know that I'm in love, and that I'm loved in return.

"Seriously, dude, you're gonna break your face."

I look up at Caleb and smile even wider, just to rub it in.

This is the first day he's been back at work with me.

He took some much needed time off last week and caught up with his dad. He's still not speaking to his mum, but I can't say I blame him. One out of two isn't bad.

I just hope that one day Everly will wake up and realise that yes, she may have lost one son, but she's got another one right here, just waiting to be loved.

"If that's what being in love looks like then I think I'll just stay single forever," he deadpans.

I know he's joking, I can see his poor attempt at hiding his smile.

The two of us haven't had a chance to really talk things out yet.

Mia told me about their talk, and I've spoken to Caleb – but not on our own like this.

I know I owe him a conversation about everything that's happened.

"One day when you find yourself a girl, and make a face like this, I'm going to pay you out so hard." I chuckle.

He shakes his head at me and grins.

"Are we good, man? I don't want shit to be weird between us," I ask, my tone serious now.

He's worked for me for a long time now. He's a hard worker, but more than that he's a friend. I like working with him every day. I'd hate for him to go.

"We're good, Luke. It's gonna take me a while to get used to it, but I can see how happy you are together, and that's all I want."

"It's not something I ever saw coming..." I look up from the framing I'm building. "I never anticipated something happening between Mia and me, but I don't know... I guess things just work out like that sometimes."

"It's just hard to get my head around... if he was here, then there would be no you and Mia. There would be Troy and Mia, and Luke and *who*? Is there someone else out there who you would have been happy with if Troy had lived?"

I shrug at him because I don't know. I'd hate to think that this was the universe's plan all along, but who am I to question the way things happen.

"It's just hard to accept that this was fate for the three of you," he says, his sentiments almost mirroring my thoughts.

I clear my throat which is feeling thick with emotion all of a sudden. I wasn't quite prepared for such a deep and meaningful. "I'm sorry I didn't get to tell you about it myself, but I'm not sorry for it happening; I could never apologise for loving her."

"I know you're not, and I wouldn't want you to be sorry... I think I can get used to there being a Luke and Mia."

"Good. Because it's going to be that way for a long time."

"I hope so, man." He picks up his measuring tape and runs it down the length of the timber he needs to cut. "Mia deserves to be happy and settled. So do you. You've both been through a lot."

"You deserve to be happy too, Caleb."

He nods his head. "Yeah... and I'm getting there."

He is. We all are. I can see it. I know everybody always says that time heals all wounds, but I never really believed it.

I wouldn't say I'm healed – I know Mia and Caleb aren't either – and maybe we never will be, but we're doing our best. The patch over the hole in my heart is holding for now at least.

We work together in comfortable silence for about half an hour before he speaks again.

"I wasn't sure if I should say anything or not, but I figure it can't hurt."

I tap the nail right in and pause. "I'm listening."

"You know that big old place for sale down on Juliet Street?"

"Yeah, I know it." I nod.

"Mia gave it 'the look' when we were out walking."

I don't have to ask him what he's means by 'the look'. I already know. I've seen that wistful look in her eyes when she's looking at something she wants or loves. I've seen that look a lot over the years. I see it when she looks at me now.

"Noted," I say with a nod.

He chuckles and goes back to his work.

***

"Do you mind staying until he's asleep?" Mia asks in a hushed tone.

She looks really nervous about asking the question and I don't understand why.

I'm here and she knows I'd never turn down an opportunity to put Joe to bed, and I'm even less likely to race off home the minute he's gone down – that's when I get my alone time with her.

"Of course I'll stay."

She smiles, but I can still see her nerves. "I know it's not Tuesday... I thought you might have other plans."

It might not be my usual night to come over, but she doesn't seem to understand that I'd be here every single night of the week if that wouldn't be classed as coming on too strong.

"The only plans I have right now are with you and Joe."

"Okay, well thank you," she whispers.

"Night, buddy," I tell him, and he waves to me.

"Night, Wuke."

I can't help smiling when he says my name. He's seriously the cutest kid.

Mia takes my hand in hers and leads me down the stairs.

I watch her bustle around in the kitchen, taking twice as long to make a cup of tea than she usually would.

She catches me watching her and winces. "What? Is Joe calling out?"

Joe hardly ever calls out after he's put to bed, the little guy usually goes out like a light, but right now Mia is acting like a cat on a hot tin roof.

"I haven't heard a peep from him. What's going on, Mia? Is something wrong?"

She shoots me a sheepish look.

"He's been playing up at bed time and crying in the mornings."

I can feel my heart rate speed up in concern. This kind of thing isn't like Joe.

"*Why*? Is he sick?"

She shakes her head and bites down on her lip. She's nervous as hell and I can't figure out what's going on.

"No."

"Nightmares?"

She shakes her head.

I cross the room and grip her elbows so she can't get away from having this conversation.

"Seriously, sweetheart, what the hell is going on? I'm getting worried."

"It's *you*," she breathes, and I can physically see the weight being lifted off her shoulders. "He's upset if you're not here to put him to bed and he cries if he wakes up and you're not there."

"Oh, *Mia*... Why didn't you tell me sooner? How long has this been happening?"

She blushes bright red. "You only went back home, what, a week ago? It started right after you stopped sleeping over..."

She's dipped her head to avoid my eyes.

"*Mia*, you didn't have to keep this from me. You know I hate seeing Joe upset as much as you do." I tip her chin up with my thumb. "You're allowed to ask me for help."

"I know I can..." She fidgets nervously. "But I didn't know *how* to ask you to be here *every* night *and* every morning..."

I can feel my heart thumping in my chest.

"Do *you* want me to be here every night and every morning?"

"I don't want you to be anywhere else," she whispers.

I search her eyes for a clue that she's only doing this for her son, but I don't find any.

"You know I'd do anything for Joe, but I can't move in with you just because he's upset... If we're going to do this it has to be because you want it, Mia. *You*. If you're not sure or you're not ready then we'll find another solution, okay?"

"I don't want another solution," she replies after a beat.

I don't want another solution either.

I've known Mia for nearly half my life. I've been here almost every day for more than two years already. I've been in love with her for a long time now.

We might not have been official for long, but it's not like she's some random woman I picked up at the pub on a Friday night.

She's Mia.

She's mine. Where either of us lives is just a minor detail at this point.

"What about if I were to pack a bag and we'll just see how it goes?" I offer.

"I already know how it's going to go, Luke. Once you sleep next to me, you'll never go back. I'm never going to want you to go."

She doesn't look nervous anymore, in fact if anything, she looks eager, but I'm wary. Not of living with her, but of pushing her too hard, too fast.

I don't want her to wake up one day and regret a thing about our life together.

So, even though she's probably right, and I will never go back, I still want to give her that out if she decides she wants to take it.

"I'll pack a big bag." I chuckle.

"A huge one." She giggles.

I kiss her forehead and try to step away, but she grips me tighter.

"Where are you going?"

"I'm going to pack the biggest god damn bag I can find, and then I'm coming right back, so you better clear me out a drawer or something, alright?"

Her face breaks out into the most beautiful smile and she claps her hands together gleefully.

"On it." She grins as she presses up to her tippy toes to kiss my lips quickly, before turning on her heel and running off upstairs.

Seeing how excited she is, I know she's right. The only way I'll leave this place is if she and Joe are coming with me.

I make my way out the front door and a picture of Mia and Troy catches my eyes from the wall. He's everywhere in their home and that's exactly how I want it to be.

I'd like to make Mia my wife someday, but she'll always have been *his* wife first.

I'll happily be a father to Joe, but I'll never let him forget who his first dad was.

I smile at the photo and walk out the door.

CHAPTER TWENTY-THREE

Mia
Three months later

"Mia?" I hear Luke's voice calling me from out back.

I stroll through the kitchen and out the back door and into the yard.

I laugh as I see what my boys have been up to out here. They've converted the yard into a football pitch, with one of the goals that Joe got for his birthday at each end.

"This yard is too small, Mia," Luke tells me as Joe picks up the ball and makes his attempt to run for the goal.

"No hands!" Luke fakes outrage. "Ref? He's been doing it all day!" He looks at me.

I shrug and giggle.

Joe runs right into the goal with the ball before throwing his hands up in victory.

Luke makes a show of falling to the ground in defeat.

"Surely that's a violation of the rules," he groans.

"I win!" Joe announces as he jumps on top of Luke.

"Urrggh," Luke moans. "Watch the twig and berries, little man."

I cover my mouth in an attempt to hide my laughter.

Joe hops up and runs off to his sandpit without a care in the world.

"Seriously, Mia, we need more space," Luke tells me from his spot in the middle of the lawn.

I wander over to him and lower myself down on top of him.

He smiles up at me and wraps his arms around me.

I kiss him and hear Joe applauding from his sandpit.

We both laugh. He's done that ever since Luke moved in. He claps every single time he sees us kissing.

It's cute and all but I hope it's not going to continue forever. He did it in the park the other day and all the other parents thought it was hilarious. I've never blushed so hard in my entire life.

The last thing I want is for people to stare at us again.

The scandal of Luke and I has finally died down now, and I'm glad.

It's not as though I particularly cared what the other mums from the music group thought, or that I was all that interested in what the neighbours might say, but I don't like being the centre of attention in the slightest, so I'm glad that we're old news now.

We still get looks everywhere we go, but I've got a strong suspicion that it has more to do with the handsome man who's constantly touching me, than it has to do with the fact that we're a couple.

"More space you reckon?" I ask as I push the hair back from his forehead.

He nods. "Need some more bedrooms for all those babies you plan on giving me."

He's got a cheeky grin on his face, but I'm more than happy for him to tease me. I might not be game enough just yet, but I do want kids with him one day.

I want a whole bunch of them.

"Well, it's lucky I booked us a viewing of that house around the corner then…" I reply.

"You *didn't*?" He's gaping at me and I wonder if I've made a mistake by doing this without talking to him first.

"I did…"

"I booked us one too," he replies sheepishly, his surprised expression morphing into a wide smile.

I laugh. That is classic us. We're so in sync sometimes it's almost scary.

"When is your appointment?" he asks.

"Today at three. You?"

"Tomorrow at nine." He chuckles. "She said she couldn't get me in today because she was showing someone else through."

"Smart lady." I wink at him.

"So, we're really doing this then? Looking for a new place… together?"

I giggle. "It sounds like we're doing it twice."

"God, I love you," he breathes.

I know he does. I really, really do. I'll never be one of those women who are never sure where they stand with their partner. I know exactly how important I am to Luke.

"I love you too." I place a quick kiss to the tip of his nose and jump up off him.

He groans as I tug on his hands, making a half ass attempt to help him stand up.

"C'mon, stinky, we've got a house to view and you need a shower."

***

"Mia?" I hear Luke call out. "What happened to that little night light thing you had out here?"

I lean against the doorway and watch his confused expression as he stares at the power socket that it used to plug into.

"It's gone."

"What happened to it?"

I throw the face cloth I'm holding into the washing basket and shrug. "I don't need it anymore... I've got you now."

I see Luke's eyes soften and I know he realises exactly how much of a big deal this is for me. That night light has been a comfort for me ever since Joe was born.

I got it for the night feeds, but then after that, I just couldn't face the empty nights without it. I felt too alone, and it frightened me.

"The darkness isn't scary anymore," I explain, and I can feel myself blush.

The smile that crosses his face is so beautiful and satisfied that I hear myself sigh in contentment.

He's everything I need and everything I want. He's the sweetest man who treats me like a princess every day. He still buys me flowers every single Tuesday and he looks at me as though he just can't quite believe his luck. I feel the same way about him.

He tips his head towards the bed and I'm more than happy to follow his lead.

"So what's the verdict on this house?" I ask him as I climb under the covers.

It's been for sale for a long time, and I know how much work it's going to be for us, but I love everything about it. I want it to be where we raise our family.

"I want to get into the ceiling space and climb up on the roof tomorrow, but I think we'd regret it if we didn't buy that house, Mia. You light up when you walk in the door."

We both roll onto our sides so we're facing one another. Even in this dim light I can see the sparkle in his gorgeous blue eyes.

I know I'll regret it if we don't buy that place – I've admired it forever – and Luke would be the perfect person to take it on. He'd restore that house with the love and tenderness the old girl deserves.

"I really want it," I whisper.

It's not like me to just come out and say what I want, but with Luke's encouragement, I'm learning that I can ask for things... That what *I* want is important.

"Then it's yours," he replies simply, as though it's nothing more than a pair of shoes from the store.

"*Ours*," I correct him.

It's terrifying – the idea of intertwining our lives to this degree after only a few short months, but at the same time, it feels like this is the right step for the three of us. Luke, Joe and I.

"Ours." He grins.

"You sure you're up for it?"

"I've never been afraid of a little hard work, Mia."

I sigh in relief and snuggle against his firm chest.

Truer words have never been spoken.

CHAPTER TWENTY-FOUR

Luke
Six weeks later

"Luke?" I hear Mia call from somewhere upstairs.

"Down by the front door," I call back.

We're going to have to get walky-talkies or something so we can find each other in this place.

Mia really wasn't wrong when she referred to this house as 'big'. She wasn't wrong about it being 'old' for that matter either, but I love it. It's got character and charm.

I've got a list of jobs longer than my arm, but that's all part of it.

We knew what we were getting into when we took this house on and we'll get through all these renovations at one point or another.

We've got a long life ahead of us to work through it.

"Where did you put that box with the towels..." Her voice trails off as she comes up behind me and sees what I'm doing.

"*Luke*," she breathes.

I straighten the last of the frames I'm hanging and step back to admire my work.

Much like everything in this house will be, this photo wall is a mix of mine and hers.

There're photos of me, Mia, Joe, Em, my parents, Caleb... and of course, Troy. In fact, the photo she admired in my bedroom from our teenage years is right here in the middle, front and centre.

"I told you I'd share that one with you one day." I point at the image I know will have caught her eye.

"You did," she replies quietly as she comes to stand in front of me.

I wrap my arms around her middle and rest my chin on her shoulder.

"This is our family," I tell her.

"Thank you for accepting *every* part of it," she whispers.

"Always, Mia."

There was never a choice. I was never going to erase Troy to make way for myself. Best friend or total stranger... that was *never* happening. I've never been the kind of guy who wants something at the expense of someone else.

"I wasn't sure you'd want pictures of him in our new home... But I'm glad you do."

"I think this is all he would have wanted from us, you know?" I say quietly.

She looks up at me in question.

"To be remembered."

She nods silently, but the green depths of her eyes say so much more.

"The towels are in a box in the living room," I say after we stare at each other for what feels like an eternity.

She places a kiss to my jaw and slips out of my arms.

I glance back up at the pictures and smile, my eyes ending up on that one special image in the middle.

"I'm doing my best to look after them," I whisper at the picture of him frozen in time. "I know it's not what you probably had in mind... But I love them, Troy. More than anything in the world. I'll look after them forever. I promise you."

I turn and walk into the heart of our home, feeling more at peace than I have in a long, long time.

EPILOGUE

Luke

"Higher, Dad, higher!" Joe yells at the top of his lungs.

It was his fourth birthday when he asked me if he could call me 'dad'. It was quite possibly the proudest moment of my whole life.

It's nearly official now too. The adoption process has been a bit of a lengthy one, but it's nearly over.

He'll officially be my son then.

It seems too good to be true – my life.

I've got a beautiful wife who's thrilled she went back to school and got her degree, and an incredible son. We have an amazing home, a crazy dog and plans to extend our family.

We've certainly been having a lot of fun practising.

"I think that's high enough, Joe," Mia calls from her spot on the picnic blanket.

"Just a little higher, Dad?" he pleads with me as he flies back and forth on the swing, a huge grin on his face.

He's an absolute daredevil this kid. He must have inherited that trait from Troy, because he sure as hell didn't get it from his mother.

I give in and push him just a tiny bit higher, hoping Mia won't notice. I hate saying no to Joe. I'm such a sucker for my little boy.

He grins at me and whoops in excitement.

It's a beautiful summer's day and the park is so busy, there are people everywhere.

It's one of Joe's favourite places to go and we're here nearly every weekend.

A middle-aged woman I don't recognise smiles as she approaches me by the swings. She hasn't got a kid with her, but there's about one hundred running around so she could have come with any one of them.

"He's gorgeous," she says as she looks at Joe. "Is he your only child?"

"Not for long if I have anything to do with it," I say with a grin.

She laughs and points to the two dog tags that I still wear around my neck most days.

One of them is mine, and one was Troy's.

"You're military?"

"Ex-army." I nod.

"You lost someone?" she prompts.

I nod. "My best friend."

I give Joe another push to keep him moving.

It still hurts when I talk about Troy, but I've learnt that not talking about him hurts more.

"I'm sorry," she says. I know she's a total stranger, but she seems awfully genuine. "I was just here with my nieces and I couldn't help but notice you... You're a very attractive guy."

I can feel myself blush. I decide that mentioning the fact that I have a wife is probably a good idea at this point, even though this woman is at least fifteen years my senior.

"Ah, um... thanks... We're just here with my wife..."

MR. MARCH

She smiles wide. "Oh goodness, I'm sorry, I'm not hitting on you... Although you seem like a total sweetheart..."

I chuckle somewhat nervously and look at her expectantly. I can't figure out what it is she wants from me.

"I normally have my photographer with me while I'm recruiting; makes it less *weird*," she replies, seeming flustered. "But I couldn't let this opportunity pass me by..."

I still haven't got the faintest idea what she's talking about, so I give Joe another push while I wait for her to spit it out.

"I'm sorry, I'm rambling... I'm the organiser of a calendar, kind of like a hot local men type of thing... and I'm looking for a Mr. March," she finally says.

I glance around to check she's not talking to someone else. "*Me?*"

"Yes *you*." She laughs. "I think you'd be perfect." She makes a gesture with her hands as though she's reading some type of banner. "*The sweetheart soldier.*"

I shake my head in disbelief, but I can't help grinning; it's flattering if not a little insane sounding.

"I'm not a soldier anymore."

She waves her hand dismissively. "That's not important."

She rummages around in her pocket and takes out a business card. "Take my number and have a think about it. Talk to your wife." She winks at me.

Sceptical as I am, I take the card from her outstretched hand and look down at it as she walks away.

"Oh and..." She frowns as she realises she doesn't know my name.

"Luke," I provide for her.

"*Luke*. Keep the beard."

I chuckle as she turns and disappears.

"Who's that lady, Dad?" Joe asks as his swing slows down to a stop.

"I'm not sure, bud." I glance at the card again and chuckle. "I'm not sure..."

OTHER TITLES

Love like Yours Series
Rushed – Book 1
Pierced – Book 2
Hunted – Book 3
Chased – Book 4

Rock Games Novels
Paper, Scissors, Rock: Vol. 1
Hide and Seek: Vol. 2

My Heart Duet
My Heart Needs
My Heart Wants

Calendar Boys Novels
Mr. January
Mr. February
Mr. March

ACKNOWLEDGEMENTS

The songs that inspired this book – I'm Yours –The Script, and Remember Me – Gavin James.

I hope you all enjoyed reading Luke and Mia's story – they're very different characters to the first two books in this series, so I hope you enjoyed reading about their love.

Thanks as always to my editors – Spell Bound – Stacey and Trina. And a big thanks to my support crew, Stacey for the daily chats and bouncing ideas, Bianca for all the BETA reading and support, Marnie, Kylee, Trish, Margaret, Robyn and all the girls in my street team for sharing my stuff all over the internet, and Lauriel for catching any little mistakes that might get through as well as sharing – I appreciate you all so much!

ABOUT THE AUTHOR

NICOLE S. GOODIN is a romance author and mother of two from Taranaki in the North Island of New Zealand.

In mid-2015, she started to write about a group of characters who wouldn't get out of her head. Her first book, Rushed, was published in mid-2016.

Nicole enjoys long walks on the beach, pillow fights and braiding her friends' hair. She dislikes clichés, talking about herself in the third person, and people who don't understand her sense of humour.

Please feel free to contact her either via her website, email, Instagram, Twitter or on her Facebook page, she would love to hear your feedback. If you're feeling really game, you can even sign up for her newsletter.

Visit www.nicolegoodinauthor.com for more information.

UPCOMING TITLES

Calendar Boys Novels

Mr. April
Mr. May
Mr. June
Mr. July
Mr. August
Mr. September
Mr. October
Mr. November
Mr. December

www.ingramcontent.com/pod-product-compliance
Lightning Source LLC
Chambersburg PA
CBHW030437010526
44118CB00011B/670